SEVEN THINGS
THAT MAKE OR BREAK
A RELATIONSHIP

7 Things That Make or Break a Relationship

FREE AUDIO & VIDEO DOWNLOADS

SEE REVERSE FOR YOUR PERSONAL CODE

For more information on Paul McKenna and his books,
see his website at www.paulmckenna.com

www.penguin.co.uk

SEVEN THINGS THAT MAKE OR BREAK A RELATIONSHIP

•

PAUL McKENNA Ph.D.

EDITED BY HUGH WILLBOURN Ph.D.

BANTAM PRESS

TRANSWORLD PUBLISHERS
61–63 Uxbridge Road, London W5 5SA
www.penguin.co.uk

Transworld is part of the Penguin Random House group of companies
whose addresses can be found at global.penguinrandomhouse.com

First published in Great Britain in 2020 by Bantam Press
an imprint of Transworld Publishers

A CIP catalogue record for this book
is available from the British Library.

ISBN 9781787632240

Typeset in 11/17pt Palatino by Julia Lloyd Design
Printed and bound in Great Britain by Clays Ltd, Elcograf S.p.A.

Penguin Random House is committed to a sustainable
future for our business, our readers and our planet. This book
is made from Forest Stewardship Council® certified paper.

1 3 5 7 9 10 8 6 4 2

CONTENTS

For Kate, you complete me!

INTRODUCTION

This book is for everyone who wants a happy relationship that gets better and more rewarding over time. Each of the following chapters has one focus and asks one question. When you have read the whole book, you can ask yourself each of the questions every day. Your answers will give your own unique insights, showing you how much easier it is than you ever thought to change your relationship for the better.

Reading the book is just one part of the process of making your relationship richer, deeper and more rewarding. There are also exercises, techniques and a hypnotic trance. You can download the trance, along with a video guide to Havening (see page 114) and audio guides to all the techniques, from www.paulmckenna.com/downloads

This combination of elements is based on a breakthrough in our understanding of relationships. The whole system helps you make positive changes at every level of your thinking and behaviour. If you want to understand what works and what doesn't, this is for you.

This system will give you the edge. It works on both your conscious and unconscious mind. The techniques will recode the habits of your conscious mind. The more you practise them, the more swiftly you will get positive change. The hypnotic trance installs complementary processes in your unconscious mind. This means that every effort you make is supported and amplified by your unconscious mind. You will begin to see yourself, the people around you, and the whole world differently.

The system works even for people who had given up hope. I have worked with people who thought they would never find a partner, and who have gone on to transform their lives in just a few months.

Relationship that are stuck in negativity cause suffering and sadness. You can say goodbye to all that. In my experience, and that of millions and millions of other humans, a rich, rewarding relationship is one of the greatest sources of happiness in the world. I sincerely want you to use the process and the techniques in this book. In doing so, you will take giant strides towards experiencing the deep, rich, long-lived happiness of a rewarding relationship at the centre of your life.

The whole system

As I have been writing this book, people have kept asking me, 'What are the seven things?' as though they were seven ideas or a checklist like you find in a popular magazine. But this book is not a list of 'must do this' or 'don't do that'. This book is not a manual of advice. It is your guide to seven *processes* of personal change. You do not need faith or blind belief to use this book, the techniques and the audio track. In fact, you don't need to believe anything at all. All you have to do is to follow the instructions and embrace the process of discovery. You will find in yourself powers to make changes you thought were impossible. If relationships, or lack of relationships, have made you feel bad in the past, you can look forward right now to a more fulfilling future. By starting to read the book, you have already begun the process of transformation. You will develop your own insights as you carry on.

I am not trying to install my model of happiness in other people. You are the expert on you, and your answers will lead you to your personal version of a deeply rewarding relationship.

This book has not been arrived at easily. I always try to make my books a system that changes people for the better. It has taken longer to research and write this book than any other book I have written.

There is now a large body of scientific research that reveals the patterns of thinking and behaviour that cause relationship problems and, more importantly, the patterns that sustain rewarding relationships. This book uses the latest scientific evidence, and I also share some of my own experience. I had to make an awful lot of mistakes in my life, over and over again for many years, to learn enough to write this. Ultimately, I discovered that relationships are the biggest game in town, so I truly hope this book gives you the greatest riches in life: a wonderful relationship!

Seven processes

The seven things that will make or break a relationship are not objects or ideas. They are activities or processes in seven specific areas. If I ask you, 'What is the first thing you do in the morning?', your reply will describe an action – something you do. As you go through this book, you will find the seven things to do that make your relationship better and better. When you have found out your own way to do them, you can continue to use them long after you have finished this book.

The processes lie in the following seven areas and in each of them your own insights will be unique:

1. Communication
We start with communication. We all do it, all the time, so better communication is one of the quickest wins in every relationship.

2. Action

Your relationship is *what happens*. And you can make it happen better every day.

3. Self-care

One of the most understandable errors people make is to think of their partner but not themselves. We explore how to care properly for both sides of the relationship.

4. Generosity

Love can be understood in many ways, but all of them should include giving. We find the kind of giving that really helps.

5. Disagreement

Some disagreement is not only inevitable, it is vital. We look at how we can do it in a good way.

6. Learning

In the best relationships we learn something every day. We can learn about our partner, our relationship, our environment and ourselves.

7. Vision of the future

The energy of a relationship flows best when it moves towards destinations that inspire us. A vision of the future shared with your partner helps you in hard times and in good times.

Core

The core of the system is answering the questions in each of the seven areas, supported by the techniques and the audio and video downloads. The book is written in such a way as to help you make the most of all its elements. The ideas and stories are fuel to help you build and deepen your relationship.

The seven questions point you towards the seven processes. In conjunction with the other elements, they will help to redirect your thinking. As you use this system, you are enriching your ability to relate to people. You will understand more clearly how to be successful in relationships and how to make sure that you are understood.

This book is not just an interesting read. It is not just a book either. It is a system, and when you use it properly it will deliver a unique benefit to your life.

HELPING PEOPLE

For years I have been helping people to achieve their goals. In seminars and in personal consultations I have talked to hundreds of thousands of people, and I have learnt something from all the people with whom I have worked.

I always admire people who are willing to ask for assistance. It takes some courage to admit you could do with a bit of help. And it takes double the courage to ask for help with your relationship because nowadays we are surrounded by images and stories of glossy, happy couples leading picture-perfect lives. So I congratulate you, right now, for investing your time in this book.

Fears and worries

Some people desperately want to be in a relationship but they feel they just don't know how to do it. Others are how I used to be: I could start a relationship but I could not get it to last.

Some people struggle with their relationship. They know they love each other, but they fight and argue too much. Other people worry about their relationship; they wish it was better or they wonder if it is the best they can do. Some are frightened of leaving, others are frightened of staying. Many people love their partners but feel stuck in a rut that is boring and unfulfilling. Many others feel they are not able to make themselves understood. If you are in any of these groups, this book is for you.

Relationships are at the centre of our lives, yet so many of us believe we could be doing them better. Often the truth is we can. However you rate your relationship now – brilliant or good or struggling – you can make it better, starting today.

If you are single right now, this system allows you to make the changes you need to make your next relationship richer, stronger and more rewarding.

Programming

We all inherit ideas and habits we have not consciously or deliberately chosen. Sometimes, we create habits to protect ourselves, and later on find that those same habits cause problems. When I was a young man, I had my heart broken, so my unconscious mind began preventing me from getting really close to anyone. It was a form of self-protection. I wasn't deliberately trying to wreck my relationships. My mind was repeating that protective action over and over again, even when perhaps I no longer needed it. It was programmed into my behaviour. This problem and others like it occur for all of us. It is not your fault. It is the fault of your programming. One of the basic purposes of the unconscious mind is to protect us. We find ourselves doing things that may not make sense at a conscious level but are driven with a powerful and compelling urgency by the unconscious mind.

A major function of this book and this system is to help you improve your psychological software. For many people just one small change is all that is necessary to release them from negative patterns. It could be that just one technique, one idea or one story is enough to dismantle your difficulties and empower you to make spectacular progress. I don't know if that is you, but I do know it is worth reading and using all the exercises and techniques and listening to the trance (see page 26) because there is no upper limit to how good your relationship can be.

The right moves

The three staple topics of women's magazines for more than fifty years have been fashion, weight loss and relationships. Magazines love to create checklists and quizzes that give instant answers and very simple advice, and TV shows have features offering soundbite wisdom. We get advice from all sides these days – from family, from friends, from the internet. Some of it is obvious, some of it is ridiculous. There is no shortage of people willing to tell you what to do. I'm sure if you look carefully you can even find some parts of this book that look like advice. But even if it is there, it is not the most important part of the book.

I have nothing against advice. If it works, use it! But it seems to me that there is something missing. The key to change is not *knowing* what to do – it is actually *doing* it, and even more importantly, doing it *when you really need it*.

This system is set up to make it as easy as possible for you to *do* something positive for your relationship every day. It doesn't have to be big, it doesn't have to be hard work, but one action every day, however small, moves you closer and closer to the rewards you are seeking. Day by day, the more you do, the more you are able to do.

The reprogramming of your unconscious mind will help you make the right moves at the right time to steer you through difficulties and enhance the backdrop of happiness in your life.

Use all the elements of this system with your full commitment and you will achieve more than you ever could by just reading advice.

Surprise

Many years ago, I was talking to my publisher and he asked me, 'Paul, can you write a book on relationships? It's a popular category.'

I replied, 'Sure – if I can stay in one!'

At that time, I couldn't do it. One after another, my relationships came to an end. In 2004, I did an interview, which you can still find on the internet, when I told the interviewer

I was 'commitment phobic'. Eight years later, in 2012, I was still saying the same thing. I told another interviewer, 'I'm not built for relationships.'

I didn't have a problem getting together with women, but it always seemed to come to an end in the same way. I began to ask myself the question, 'Why do I keep dating people and so often it ends the same way?'

One day, a good friend pointed out to me that the common denominator in all my relationship problems was me. The women were who they were. If I wanted them to behave differently, or if I wanted a different type of person to like me, the person who needed to change was me. That conversation had a powerful effect on me. Later, I was to discover that even more powerful changes were at work.

Pleasure

When people talk to me about their relationships, I think about the difference between pleasure and happiness. I ask myself, 'What is this person's motivation? Are they seeking pleasure or are they seeking happiness?'

Pleasure is all about sensation and gratification. Pleasure is having good feelings right now. Pleasure is a bar of chocolate or glass of champagne. For some people it is an afternoon gardening, for others it is a bicycle ride. It can be going to a concert, going out for dinner or going on holiday.

Pleasure is one of the biggest drivers of human behaviour. I like pleasure! We should all have plenty of it in our lives. However, there are two myths about pleasure that we need to bust. The first is that with enough time and money you can have infinite amounts of pleasure. It turns out that however much money you have and whatever experiences you can buy, sooner or later the pleasure will cease to amuse you unless you also have happiness with it.

The prize is happiness

The second myth is that the more pleasure you have, the happier you will be. That's not true. Scientific studies have shown that lottery winners get very happy when they win their prize, but one year later their level of happiness is the same as before they won.

Money can buy pleasure, but happiness is an inside job.

Happiness is not the result of accumulated pleasurable experiences. Happiness is completely different. Happiness is the reward for living in accordance with your deepest values. Happiness is having a positive and rewarding emotional landscape to your life. Happiness comes not just from what you feel but from moving towards your goals and living your values. In a happy relationship you share goals and values with another person and move towards them together. There is nothing wrong with pleasure and enjoying the sensations of life. However, it turns out that something more is necessary for long-term happiness. A long-term relationship can provide the shared values and companionship that make life more deeply rewarding and the pleasures even sweeter.

My friend General Graham Lamb once said to me, 'There are ultimately only two big decisions in life: "Who are you going to partner with?" and "How are you going to die?" The rest is noise.'

The answers to these two questions ultimately will determine your happiness. Your partner will be the most influential and important person in your life. Whoever that person is, he or she will bring new possibilities to your life. How you are going to die determines how you live. If you want to die happy in old age you have to start being happy and healthy now. Improving your relationships is one of the most powerful ways to protect your health and improve your overall happiness.

CLARITY

If you are seeking a relationship, or seeking to improve a relationship, it helps to be very clear about what you are looking for or the changes you want to see. If you put vagueness out, you get vagueness back. On the other hand, being clear about what you want can have almost miraculous consequences.

Whenever I work with someone the first question I ask is, 'What do you want?'

A woman I know once told me that to fill time while waiting for a flight she wrote out a detailed list of the things she wanted in a man. All her points were an expression of her values. Soon afterwards, she met her ideal guy. He matched all the points on her list, right down to putting the toilet seat down after he used it. They have been happily married for years now.

Many, many other people have done similar exercises with similar results. Of course, there are other stories about people who never get into relationships because they are far too picky. So what should we do? Write a list of every required attribute, like choosing the options on a new car? The power of writing the list is that it focuses your attention. What matters most is not the items on the list but the values behind them. As we will see later, values are more significant than details.

Whether or not the specific details get matched, it is

really helpful to be clear about what you value because your values help you recognize and choose the person who is right for you.

Two perspectives

Every relationship involves two people and hence two perspectives. If you have a partner who reads this book, he or she will read this from their own perspective, which differs from yours. That is not a problem. That is a benefit. As you discuss your different interpretations, you find out more about your own perspectives and beliefs, and your partner's. Very often, I find these simple questions help people discover that they have been driven by beliefs of which they were unaware. As they become conscious of those beliefs, they get to choose whether they want to keep them or not. If you read this book with your partner, it will help you bring out the best version of yourself and the best version of your partner.

If you are currently single, or you feel that the same mistakes keep happening every time you start a relationship, you can still answer the questions, and the process will help you explore new and more rewarding ways to relate to a partner.

Uniqueness

Every relationship is unique, so how come there are seven things that make or break them? The answer is that we all face the same challenges. It is like a hand-written diary. Everyone who writes by hand uses some sort of pen or pencil, and yet what each person writes in their diary is unique.

The seven questions in this book are tools to help you to find your own way towards a rich, rewarding, successful relationship, just as a pen or pencil is a tool for you to write your own unique thoughts.

The price of success is the willingness to put some energy into your relationship every day. I am here every step of the way with the questions to help you and the tools you need to find your unique answers.

At the start of each chapter I will ask a question and I invite you to answer it in any way you wish. There is no 'right' answer or 'wrong' answer. Remember you are the expert on you. Your answers and the rest of the chapter will give you the material you will work with to improve your relationship.

How it works

At the end of each chapter we will summarize the makers and breakers we have discussed, and we will ask the question again. I'd like you to write down your own answer to the question each time you ask it. You can do so here, in the book, or in your own notebook if you prefer. Please do actually write down your answer. Research has demonstrated conclusively that we are far more likely to pay attention to ideas we have written down than to ideas that are just noted in our minds.

You will find that as you go through the process of the book, your own personal answer to each question evolves. These are not questions with a single answer. They are questions you can ask every day, and each day you will find a new answer.

Seven steps to happiness

You can use the seven questions in this book every day. As you read through the book now and follow the instructions, you lay the foundations for a richer, more rewarding intimacy with your partner. You can go as slowly or quickly as is best for you. Occasionally you have to put in a bit of thought or energy, but before you finish the book you will find that the rewards are already flowing in. You can look forward to better times, to enjoyable excitement and peaceful happiness. Start right now to give yourself the best relationship possible!

THE WHOLE PROCESS

The next seven chapters of this book are about to give you what you want. As I explained earlier, the seven things are not objects or lessons to learn, but seven processes that will transform you and your life for the better. Whether you are merely intrigued or outright amazed, everything is about to get better. You don't have to remember every single detail straightaway. Just by reading it you are taking it into your unconscious mind, and you will find that you come back and pick up this book again to remind your conscious mind of details when you need them.

This book works on two levels, on the conscious and unconscious mind. The conscious mind is the mind we actively think with, the one that we talk to ourselves with, all day long. The unconscious mind is the larger mind that you are mostly unaware of. It keeps our heart beating and controls all our automatic behaviours and is your source of wisdom and self-revelation. By practising the exercises and techniques you add them to the resources of your unconscious mind, and the hypnotic trance boosts all of those resources and makes them easier to use.

Why does this work so well?

Sometimes people tell me, 'I have read your book and it was interesting.' I then ask if they did the techniques, and sometimes they say, 'No, I didn't get around to that.' I then suggest they would have been better off just doing the techniques and not reading a single word of the narrative. They usually look a little surprised at this point. This bold statement is to put things in perspective. In truth, they would have been best doing both! When you engage your whole mind, conscious and unconscious, you suddenly become the major shareholder in your own destiny and life. So, please, don't just read the text, please use the whole system. I spent a long time crafting and testing it. As well as reading the menu, please also taste the food.

THE TRANCE

If you have not yet done so, please listen to the hypnotic trance as soon as it is safe and convenient for you to do so. Find a time and a place where you are free to pay attention to it completely. Do not listen to it while you are doing anything else. Choose a time when you can be undisturbed for 30 minutes. Many people choose to listen to my trances at night as they fall asleep. If you do so, you might wake up out of the trance and then go to sleep as normal, or you might fall straight into refreshing sleep.

Please use the trance every day for one week to install and strengthen all the positive changes to improve your relationship.

After the first week, use the trance as often as you wish to enjoy the relaxation and to continue enhancing your relationship.

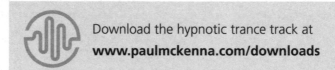

Download the hypnotic trance track at
www.paulmckenna.com/downloads

THE
WHOLE
PROCESS

COMMUNICATION

•

Q1.
HOW ARE YOU
COMMUNICATING?

Q1. HOW ARE YOU COMMUNICATING?

We have all been influenced by situations and events beyond our control. The whole environment of childhood has a long-term effect. Sometimes a single event, perhaps just a passing remark heard at a vulnerable time, can have a profound effect.

The way our parents behave is the template for how we will behave towards our partners in the future. When we see how our parents treat each other, it sets the standard for how we expect to behave and to be treated. When they are loving, that sets a template for how we are loving. I don't mean that we recreate exact copies of their movements or words. I mean that what they show us becomes our assumption about how to love and be loved.

Even though some people try to be completely different from their parents, it is as though our parents' behaviour is a training video. Often we imitate the role of our favourite parent. If that doesn't work out, we say to ourselves, 'I am never going to date someone like that again,' but our next most likely move is to imitate the role of the other parent and become the other side of the relationship.

This system will free you from that unconscious repetition. You will no longer be driven by patterns that you never chose. You can keep all the good parts of what you have inherited and the rest can just fall away.

Nowadays many of us have families that aren't just Mum and Dad. Maybe you have a stepdad or stepmum, or both.

There are lots of blended families and single-parent families and families in which several adults have been involved. Many families change and evolve over time. Whatever the situation you were brought up in, it is best to think of it as raw material. It always has some influence but it can never totally control you.

Freedom

Society has changed enormously in the last hundred years. We have now had very reliable contraception for over fifty years and it has hugely changed the way we live. It has brought us more freedom of behaviour, but it also means we have to make decisions about whether or when to have children, which our ancestors did not have to make.

Most of us now live amid many different, even conflicting, traditions. We inherit beliefs and expectations from the people who raise us. Sometimes those people have very fixed ideas of what they want us to do. At the same time, social development and travel expose us to many, many other styles of relationship. We have more choice about the gender of our partner, about the number of our partners and about how we live than ever before. More people than ever in long-term relationships choose not to live with their partner. There are now so many options that it is not easy to decide what to do.

Legal does not mean easy

Societies all over the world are moving, slowly or quickly, towards greater and greater freedom in our choice of partners. Now there is more and more legal and social equality for all types of relationship. However, although social and legal changes make all these varieties of relationship easier, they don't remove the fundamental challenges inherent in every relationship. Whatever your sex, whatever your gender, however you identify, wherever you live, an intimate relationship remains a personal challenge.

The emotional journey of a relationship has its ups and downs. You can't avoid challenging feelings. This system helps you to work through those challenges and build the intimacy and knowledge of yourself and your partner that are the core of your relationship.

The internet

After contraception and legislation, the third huge social change is digital media. The internet has changed everything. Different apps will come and go but the internet itself won't disappear. Instant communication and mass publication are here to stay.

The internet has made pornography instantly available all over the world in a couple of clicks. Porn appears to deliver an infinity of fantasy partners but it offers sexual stimulation with no actual physical contact. All the porn in the world is made of edited images. Getting to see a naked person takes less than a second on the internet. Getting to know a real person well enough to be truly intimate with them takes rather longer.

The internet has a huge impact on how we relate to each other. For example, consider how arranging social events has changed. A hundred years ago almost all events had to be arranged in advance by face-to-face invitation or by a letter. Nowadays we can send a short message: *C u 4 dinner?*

This shorthand has changed the dynamic of relationships. As we lose all the little greetings and the time taken to talk to each other, we lose all the subtle emotional signals that build our relationships. Without enough speaking and interaction to carry feeling, emotional understanding gets more difficult.

Weirdly, the internet, which has made it cheaper and easier to communicate with more people than ever, has actually made many people more lonely than before. It is a narrow channel of communication. People who text all day long can easily find they become quite shy when they wish to speak face to face. It is easier to text because you can edit what you write before you send it. Communicating online is like talking through a letterbox. It is a bigger challenge to talk face to face with a person in real life.

Exaggeration

It is tempting to exaggerate our good points a little too much, and the internet has made it way too easy. Online it is common for people to post downright lies. Some people exaggerate or lie about their age. They lie about their height. They post photos that are years old. They photoshop their waistlines and their wrinkles. They say they are self-employed when they are actually out of work and they pose with cars they don't own. Online deception is fairly pointless because unless you actually do look the same now as you did twenty years ago, when you meet your date the difference will be obvious and disappointing so you will start on a bad note. But still many people try to paint themselves as richer or cleverer or better than they really are.

If you are not willing to be honest, you can still have many relationships. You may even have lots of sex and personal and financial success. You may become rich and famous and powerful. You can achieve an awful lot without being honest, but you can never truly relax and you will never have real intimacy. You will feel like a fraud and constantly wonder if you are about to be found out. Even if you fool your lover and she or he believes every word you say, you still won't have intimacy, because you will not be able to be completely truthful about your beliefs and feelings.

Another more subtle disadvantage to being deceitful is that someone dishonest is more at risk of someone else being dishonest and taking advantage of them. Keeping up a lie takes attention and energy. A liar is always watching to see that the other person believes them, so their full attention is not available to assess the other person's honesty. There is a fair chance that liars end up with someone who is lying right back at them.

The price of true love is the same for all of us, from billionaire to pauper. The price is honesty.

The skills of socializing

One of my good friends is a true tech genius. His amazing work helps to keep our world safe. He is a wonderful, unassuming chap. We were both at a busy event where I was talking to a lot of people and, in a quiet moment, he said to me, 'That's a real skill, isn't it?'

Initially, I had no idea what he was talking about, so I asked him what he meant. With a slight hesitation, he said, 'You know, going into a room and talking to anyone you want, people you don't know, so easily! That's a real skill,' he repeated. I stopped and suddenly had a massive insight!

Up to that point, I knew some people were more outgoing than others, but I hadn't really thought about how I get on with people. I realized that what came easily to me did not come easily to everyone, and vice versa. Maybe I could make a difference to how people relate to each other.

How is it that some people seem to get on with anyone? In recent years, scientists have figured out a lot of why people get on and why they don't. It is really fascinating. By the time you finish this book, you will know a lot more about how people tick and how you can get on with them if you want, and why some people don't get on with you and how you can change that if you want. I find that as you pay attention carefully, you can see exactly how it is done and, as a result, you become a more powerful person who gets more of what they truly want.

In the 1970s, two brilliant researchers, Richard Bandler and John Grinder, spent a lot of time observing excellent communicators and, among other things, noting what they did and working out why people get on and why they don't. They codified their observations into what has now become a hugely influential template. Their breakthrough insights are used today by almost every sales person and therapist on the planet. Sadly, their insights have been distorted and repackaged by some sales trainers to become ways to manipulate people, but nothing could be further from the truth of Bandler and Grinder's original intentions. They just wanted people to understand each other better and to get along better. This chapter contains the simple but powerful core of their work, so you will know how to get on with just about anybody if you decide you want to, in future.

The real secret of how to get on with anybody

Drs Bandler and Grinder discovered that when people feel closely connected and understood, their speech and behaviour become more similar. It is not so much *what* people say, but *how* they say it, and not so much *what* they do, but *how* they do it. For example, if one person tends to talk fast and the other one slowly, as they get on better, the fast one slows down a bit and the slow one speeds up a bit. This synchronization is referred to as 'being in rapport' but in fact it happens completely naturally every day. It occurs in our body posture, movements, speed, tone and volume of speech, and the kinds of words we use.

We can use this knowledge to increase understanding of other people and help people trust us. If I make myself more similar to the person I'm talking to, their unconscious mind says, 'This person is like me – I can trust them.' Numerous books have been written about rapport by many psychologists and therapists, but we can sum up the essence in a useful way in regard to relationships very simply under these three headings: Mirroring, Reducing differences, and Focus on commonalities.

Mirroring

One scientific study showed that when people communicate, 7 per cent of the meaning is conveyed by the verbal content, 38 per cent by the tone, and 55 per cent, more than half, by the body language. For example, 'No' is one of the simplest words in the English language yet it can be said in a hundred different ways. It can be said happily, sarcastically, encouragingly and sadly. Different gestures, posture and tone can give it hundreds more meanings. It can show amazement, rejection, approval, fear and delight, and many, many other emotions.

So much more is communicated by *how* we speak than the actual words we say that there is a huge opportunity to dramatically increase rapport simply by matching the body posture and gestures of another person. This is known as 'mirroring', but it is not about trying to move or stand in an identical way, nor is it an attempt to mimic or replicate the other person. You are not trying to do exactly the same thing, because they might think you are making fun of them and that will work against you. Mirroring is much more gentle and subtle than that. It is like getting in harmony with the other person by aligning yourself with their rhythm or tone. So if someone is standing tall and upright, you can just be a bit more upright yourself. If the person you are talking to is very animated and makes a lot of gestures, you might also use your hands a bit more than usual. Mirroring works well when it is just a hint of similarity to the other person. It can be as little as leaning forward slightly, because the other person does so.

Sometimes we can have the same effect by harmonizing with a movement but using a different part of the body. If someone is making a big movement with their arms, you can echo it gently with just a hand or a finger. If they are tapping their finger on the table, you might from time to time move your foot with a similar rhythm.

When people get on well, their patterns of speech naturally begin to converge. For example, when two people meet, if one speaks quietly, the other will tend to get quieter. If one person has a very high voice, other people will tend to raise the pitch of their own voice just a little in order to get closer to them. If one person speaks very fast, the other tends to speak fast too. It is said that when lovers are sitting at a table they look like book ends, because they match each other as they lean towards each other. Rapport and mirroring are things that happen naturally when people get on with each other. We become better communicators just by doing it a little bit more.

Reducing differences

The second element of rapport is simply reducing differences. There are very straightforward versions of this. If two friends have opposing political views, they soon learn that the best way to ensure they enjoy each other's company is to avoid talking about politics. That seems obvious, but even when we do it in very small ways, it will have a positive effect. When you meet your friends and you talk about topics that you all enjoy, the energy is warm, strong and positive. If one person starts talking at length about his or her own special topic that no one else is interested in, very soon you feel the energy and the warm feeling ebb away. The closer you stay to what you have in common, the easier it is to get on with people. This is true of far more than just speech. It is even true of how you dress. For example, you may notice, while on a date, that your date has a more relaxed, informal style of dressing than you. So, if you meet a few times, you will discover that if you adopt a more relaxed style you feel more comfortable with each other. If your date likes sharp dressing and bold colours, you will find that a small move in that direction will make you both look and feel closer. Again, the goal is not imitation or looking the same, but reducing differences a little to create a sense of harmony.

Focus on commonalities

Bandler and Grinder noticed that rapport increased when people focused on what they had in common. They focused on similarities in body posture, tone, level of volume, speed of speech, use of specific language and ways of describing and perceiving the world along with core values. We all know what a nice feeling it is to discover that someone we have just met randomly knows other friends of ours. In the same way, it is a pleasure to discover that new friends share our interests, whether that is Formula One, knitting, horse-riding or karaoke. Good communicators will really pay attention. In itself it is nice to feel someone is really listening, and it encourages people to share their thoughts and enthusiasm. This allows you to focus on similarities, amplify positives and emphasize where your interests overlap.

We tend to like people who seem like us

These three elements of rapport are simple, easy and natural, yet they can be very powerful indeed. In fact, they are the key to having a good time, whether that is on a first date or a fiftieth wedding anniversary. We tend to like people who are like us. The more we perceive we have in common with someone, the easier it is to like them.

The key to success here is to be honest with yourself and the people you talk to. It is possible to flatter people by pretending to share an interest or enthusiasm, but if it is pretence, sooner or later the fakery will be exposed. Flattery is like fake money. A flatterer may fool someone at first, but sooner or later they will be found out, and after that people won't trust anything they say, because they know that the flatterer can't be trusted to give an honest opinion.

Sometimes people have questioned me at seminars and said, 'Surely this is manipulative?' There are two answers to this. The most important is intention. If your intention is honourable, that will drive the outcome. Secondly, it is not manipulative to do your very best. Communication is like any other human skill. You can do it badly, averagely or very well indeed. I think you should always do your best, and I believe rapport helps you to communicate very well indeed. I also trust you to be honourable and truthful. When you bring the focus to what you have in common, you build rapport and goodwill. When you tell the truth, you lay the foundations for trust.

PRACTISING RAPPORT

The next time you are communicating with someone, do the following:

1. Watch their posture and copy it to some degree.
2. Watch how they gesticulate, and make similar movements. If they wave their arms when they are talking, you can copy to some extent with a little movement with one of your fingers.
3. Listen to the tone and volume of their voice and try to make your own similar.
4. Listen to the speed at which they speak and make your speed similar.

Practise this gently but often until you find it happens more and more easily, and your relationships are more relaxed and closer.

STARTING A RELATIONSHIP

Some of the most fascinating research on how couples get together was conducted more than twenty-five years ago by an American researcher called Dr Timothy Perper. Dr Perper spent thousands of hours sitting in singles bars and watching men and women get together. His observations showed that there is a precise sequence of moves which predict whether or not two people would make a date and/or leave together.

The first move is non-verbal. When the two people are within speaking range, one acknowledges the other one with a nod, a smile or a glance.

The next step is verbal. One of them says, 'Hi' or some similar opening words.

Interestingly, regardless of what is said, the next vital step is again non-verbal.

If the person spoken to turns at least their head towards the speaker and acknowledges their words, a conversation will start. If, during that conversation, the parties turn more and more to face each other they are likely to make a connection. If they turn away, the likelihood of intimacy decreases.

Dr Perper's work shows how important our non-verbal communications are in emotional settings. Whether you are seeking a relationship or have been married for thirty years, something as simple and easy as turning to face your partner can help you convey more love and them to feel more loved.

A scientist called Zick Rubin became interested in how to

measure love. He devised an experiment that showed that the more people are in love, the more they engage in eye contact. He gave young dating couples a long questionnaire to assess how much they were in love and then asked them to wait for a little while for the next stage of the experiment. That wait actually was the next stage of the experiment. He observed secretly while they were waiting and measured the amount of time they gazed at each other. The higher their score on the questionnaire, the more they looked at each other.

Rubin's work is not really astonishing. After all, we can all observe how much loved-up people look at each other. What it does tell us, like Dr Perper's work, is that non-verbal signalling is vitally important. The more we let ourselves show how much we are attracted to our loved ones, the more likely it is that they will respond. The more attention we pay, the greater the window of opportunity. We really can convey an ocean of attraction with just a look or a turn of the head.

Conversation

Every relationship is a conversation. A long-term relationship is a long-term conversation. That is true both literally and metaphorically. We talk to our partners every day, over and over again for years. It is like a long conversation, interrupted by all the other things we have to do in our life. It follows that the better that conversation, the better the relationship.

What you say to each other, day in day out, has a constant effect on how you and your partner feel. Of course, as we will be exploring, there is far, far more to a relationship than the words you speak to each other, but they are a very important element. So, when you do speak, you might as well do it as well as you possibly can.

The science of what makes or breaks relationships

There is a psychologist in Seattle who can predict with 90 per cent accuracy whether or not a couple will stay together after just twenty minutes of conversation. His prediction is not guesswork but based on scientific studies. Dr John Gottman* of the Gottman Institute in Seattle has been studying relationships for forty years. In his early career, he listened to the conversations of thousands of couples and took extensive notes. He would score positive and negative comments to understand the patterns that lay beneath the everyday talk and chatter.

After many years of careful, scientific observation, he identified specific patterns of language that indicated a relationship is in trouble. He discovered that by listening for these patterns in the conversation between partners, he could

* You can find out more about Dr Gottman's work and his research at www. gottman.com

predict which couples will stay together and which couples will divorce. Dr Gottman discovered four patterns which predicted trouble.

PERSONAL CRITICISM

The first sign of trouble is personal criticism. When either party repeatedly labels the other as bad, the relationship is threatened. It is perfectly possible to disagree with someone or dislike what someone does without being critical of who they are. In other words, it is vital to distinguish between someone's identity and their actions.

For example, let us imagine Jane says, 'Let's go to Spain for our holidays next year' and John replies, 'I'm not sure about that. Maybe we should think about somewhere more local,' and Jane says, 'You are so negative!'

Jane has abandoned discussing holidays and has moved to a personal criticism of John. If the disagreement continues like this, it will be about his character, and soon or later hers, and not about the holiday. That is not likely to lead to happiness.

If Jane is frustrated, she needs to stop complaining and start looking for a solution. Telling John he is negative does not help her get the holiday she wants, *even if in fact all the evidence shows that she is correct.*

When she remembers that a person is separate from their actions, she helps both of them to find different ways for him to respond. She can ask him instead what his specific worry is or, better still, she can ask him what he would need in order to feel that Spain would be a great place to go on holiday. She could ask him why he would rather go somewhere local. Maybe he is worried about the cost, maybe he is frightened of flying. Maybe he doesn't like Spanish food. Even if his comment comes from an automatically negative frame of mind, asking questions gives him lots of opportunities to think further and modify his attitude.

Personal criticism is not always as obvious as that. Our everyday language is littered with common phrases that muddy the distinction between the person and their actions. One very unhelpful example is the question that starts, 'Why do you always . . . ?' In the case above, if Jane were to say, 'Why do you always dismiss my suggestions?' it might sound as though she is talking about actions, but actually the generalization makes it equivalent to criticizing the whole person. The word 'always' makes the action appear to be a permanent character flaw. Not surprisingly, John is likely to defend himself.

If an argument follows, more often than not the argument is about the wrong thing. Instead of finding a holiday they can both enjoy, it becomes an argument about 'always', about her criticism of his character. Even if she got an exact, complete and truthful answer to 'Why do you always dismiss my suggestions?' it wouldn't move them any closer to a nice holiday. Jane doesn't really want to know *why* John reacts negatively, she wants him to react *differently*.

Jane will get a far more useful answer if she asks, 'What sort of holiday would you like?' Then the two of them can compare their different ideas and find out where they best overlap.

DEFENSIVENESS

The second sign that Gottman identifies of a relationship in trouble is defensiveness. Defensiveness is the counterpart to criticism. If John tells Jane, 'I'm not negative, you are just unrealistic,' he defends himself and then counterattacks. Now the chances of this discussion deteriorating into an argument are very high indeed.

It is remarkable how quickly arguments can escalate when one person is critical and the other is defensive. None of us actually like being criticized but the trick is to avoid immediately fighting back. Rather than fighting back, John could ask, 'What makes you say that?' and it will give him a bit more information and a bit of time to find a way to keep talking that is neither critical nor defensive but heads towards a solution.

STONEWALLING

The third signal of danger is when one partner refuses to engage with the other. This is called 'stonewalling' or 'shutting out'. Stonewalling is a way of being nasty without overtly doing anything. This is a version of passive aggression, a form of attack that works by simply ignoring the normal social non-verbal agreements.

If John ignores Jane's holiday suggestion and says nothing, he is rejecting the invitation to speak which is implied in her words. It is as though he is shutting a door in her face. If she complains, John might say, 'Hey, what's the problem? I didn't do anything!' But of course that is the problem. Doing nothing at all is not a good option here. A relationship is like a game of tennis. It is an ongoing process. If someone stops moving, they stop playing. If they refuse to return the ball or walk off the court, they are not playing tennis any more.

It is difficult to respond well to stonewalling, but if you manage it, the rewards are great. It is better not to keep trying to engage with the stonewalling but rather to retreat and remain positive. When the other party starts to re-engage, refrain from revenge and instead focus on building understanding and moving towards positive action.

CONTEMPT

The fourth and by far the most dangerous sign of trouble is contempt. If Dr Gottman hears contempt from either partner, he knows the relationship is heading for the rocks. In some cases, the contempt is an indication that the person has already cut themselves off emotionally. They no longer care for their partner, and no longer enjoy their company. Lacking the honesty, or the courage, to leave, they stay and make their own lives and that of their partner miserable.

Contempt is being cut off emotionally by someone who no longer values the other person enough to respect them.

However, someone who is contemptuous of their partner is also indirectly insulting themselves. That is a recipe for more unhappiness. For example, if a wife is always putting her husband down and insulting him in front of her friends, she is also making herself look bad. After all, she chose her husband.

If you find yourself in the sad situation of either receiving or delivering contempt, you need to change it. It is worth using everything in this book to make a strong effort to respect and reconnect to your partner.

Unconscious rudeness

The more you think about Dr Gottman's list the more obvious it seems. It is no surprise that people will drift apart if they consistently subject each other to contempt, criticism, defensiveness and stonewalling.

If it is as obvious as that, why do I even need to mention it? Gottman's four problems are far more common than we wish *because we often don't notice we are doing them.*

Often the perpetrators think they are doing something entirely different. Some people think of it as banter; others insist it is nothing to do with the person, they are just dismissing some ridiculous ideas. People who are criticizing their partner may tell themselves that they are 'just being honest' or 'expressing feelings'. Often when a person is being contemptuous, they are feeling impatient or irritated and they are simultaneously insensitive, so they don't feel how unkind their words are. They may be saying honestly what they feel and believe, without awareness of the significance of *how* they say it. This sort of thing can happen accidentally when banter goes too far.

I don't believe people reading this book really want relationships to end. I believe you want your relationship to be functional and rewarding. Fortunately Dr Gottman's work also indicates what sort of behaviour enhances relationships.

MAKING RELATIONSHIPS WORK

Dr Gottman's research revealed four straightforward actions that are excellent predictors of a happy, long-lasting relationship. The more people did these, the greater their chances of success.

LISTENING

There are times when it is tempting to tune out when your partner is talking. After you have known them for a while you probably do know roughly what they are going to say. You know their habits and their concerns, and people do often say the same things and raise the same concerns over and over again. But listening carefully always pays dividends. It allows you to notice the small variations that tell you a lot about someone's mood and, even more importantly, listening carefully is a sign of respect. People like to feel they are being properly heard and that makes them more confident about sharing more private and intimate thoughts.

Happy couples are good at listening. They give time and attention to their partner and make an effort to understand them. That means, for example, when a partner comes home from work and wants to talk about the office politics, the other one listens. Maybe they don't know the people involved, or they think the whole business is silly and unnecessary, but the one talking wants to talk and be heard so that they can get it off their chest. Talking also helps them to think through issues. As we hear ourselves speak, we can understand our ideas better and we all appreciate the chance to do that.

RESPONDING TO BIDS

John Gottman realized that many of the actions and things we say in the daily chat in a relationship are bids for attention. If you hold out your hand to your partner as you are walking, that is a 'bid' to hold hands. It feels bad if your partner ignores it. It feels good if they take your hand and hold it. If you say 'Hello' as you come home from work, that is a 'bid' for a conversation. If all you get back is a flat 'Hello' it feels bad. If you get a warm, 'Hi there. How was your day?' it feels good. These little bids happen over and over again every day. When partners respond to them, they feel warm towards each other and the relationship is nourished.

EXPRESSING ADMIRATION

Gottman noticed that couples who get on well express their admiration for each other regularly. They have a habit of noticing beauty and kindness and complimenting each other. You may think your wife, husband or partner looks beautiful. Perhaps you even told them so last year. Well, if you still think it, your partner will definitely appreciate being told more than once a year.

EXPRESSING OPTIMISM

Happy couples pay attention to, and comment on, the good things in life. They see and share with each other good news and ordinary pleasures. They appreciate life every day. When they see or hear something nice, they share it with their partner and the pleasure is doubled.

These four actions are simple and easy. They are easy to forget when people get stressed or depressed, but the more we remember them, the better life is on a simple, everyday level. Paying attention and paying compliments are excellent habits to cultivate.

MODES OF THINKING

Bandler and Grinder, the two researchers I mentioned earlier, learned a great deal about communication from their careful observations. We all use pictures (visual), sounds and words (auditory), and feelings (kinaesthetic) to think. Bandler and Grinder observed that human beings tend to favour one mode of communication and thinking. Even though we all use all three modes throughout our communication, we tend to have a strong preference for one, and the way we communicate is strongly influenced by our preferred mode of thinking.

Expressions

People tend to use expressions that reflect their preferred mode of thinking. People with a visual preference, for example, will say things like, 'I **see** what you mean,' or, 'The future **looks** good.' They like to see things with their own eyes and they would rather see evidence than hear arguments. When I talk to them, I might refer to 'the big **picture**' or 'bringing things into **focus**'. If I want them to explain something to me I might ask, 'And what would that **look** like?' If I have to explain a complicated idea, I would try to use a diagram or picture to explain it rather than a long speech.

People with an auditory preference say things like, 'Well, that **sounds** good to me,' or, 'That **rings a bell**.' When I express agreement with auditory people, I would say something like, 'We are **singing** from the same hymn sheet.' Auditory people are sensitive to tone of voice, and when they hear someone speak, tend to be better than average at knowing whether that person is, or is not, telling the truth.

People with a kinaesthetic preference will say, 'Let's **touch** upon this,' or, 'That **feels** good.' If someone said, 'I find your ideas hard to **grasp**,' I would reply with, 'Let me give you some **concrete** examples.'

Identifying modes of thinking

Bandler and Grinder also identified a correlation between people's preferred modes of thinking and certain patterns in people's eye movement. You can discover this by noticing where people's eyes tend to move when you ask them a question. When you ask them, 'What do you remember about your childhood?', if their eyes move up, they're likely to be a visual thinker, if their eyes move sideways, they're likely to be an auditory, and if their eyes move down, a kinaesthetic.

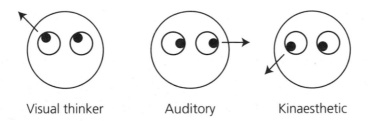

Visual thinker   Auditory   Kinaesthetic

Preferences and understanding

Preferred modes of thinking affect behaviour. Visual people look at you directly and like you to look them in the eye when you are talking. Often people with an auditory preference will look away because they are turning their ear towards you to hear better, and are looking away to the side to help themselves think clearly.

You will often find that people are in jobs that reflect their preferences. Television producers, photographers and interior designers are usually visual; singers, musicians and radio broadcasters are mostly auditory, and often builders, craftspeople and personal trainers have a kinaesthetic preference.

When you use the same type of expression as another person, they understand you more clearly. I used to work for a man who used sports metaphors all the time. He talked about 'kicking into touch', 'getting out and batting', 'winning big' and 'knocking the ball home'. When I noticed what he was doing, I started doing the same. I talked about being 'a team player' and 'running with the ball' and we got on better and better.

Don't be too surprised to find out just how powerful it can be to change your language. The same words can have a huge variety of meanings depending on the tone of voice we use. In the same way, when we change the type of expression we use, we can massively change the power of our communications.

This enhancement of your language works just as well

with your partner as it does with complete strangers. In fact, there is a double benefit. When you match the communication style of your partner, they will feel happier and better understood. At the same time, they will understand you better. Your ideas will be clearer to them when expressed in their favoured type of language. It is a simple, easy win-win.

It would be very rare to meet someone who uses expressions drawn exclusively from one mode. On the other hand, almost everyone will show a preference if you listen to them carefully for a while. You don't need to change your entire use of language. The most effective and subtle changes are gradual. As you notice your partner's preferred mode, you can introduce a few expressions that match their preferences.

THE LOVE STRATEGY

When I came across the love strategy, it totally changed my approach to relationships. It was a complete revelation. Up until then, when I was in a relationship I constantly wondered why I was trying so hard to show the other person I really cared about them and why they just didn't get how I felt. Things I said or did had no impact, no matter how hard or often I tried. They just didn't seem to get what I was trying to communicate to them. It was so frustrating. I wanted them to know how much I cared for them, but it was as though I was speaking another language.

Then I learned the love strategy and everything changed. Everything became clear and I was able to communicate how I felt and was understood. I was able to understand my partner better as well. It didn't mean I never had problems, but the arguments and frustration went away immediately, as if by magic.

I remember once I was mystified at how I seemed to cause offence even when I was being grateful. I remember being given a gift, saying thank you and then putting it aside on my desk.

'Don't you like it?'

'Of course I do,' I replied. 'I'm going to put it somewhere special later.'

'So you don't like it,' came the reply.

When I understood the love strategy, I realized that the

person who gave me that gift was visual. She expected me to look at it, to examine it, to comment on what I could see and then put it right in front of me on my desk.

It also become clear to me that my own preferred mode of thinking is auditory. I am grateful for each and every gift I am given, but I am truly touched if a person tells me they love me in an authentic and meaningful way. It is not at all surprising that my first career was in radio.

This next set of observations and the techniques that go with it are deceptively simple but are an integral part of the difference that will make all the difference in the world to you.

THE LOVE STRATEGY

Our styles of communication offer a simple but astonishingly powerful way to increase the intimacy in our relationships. Please read the exercise through from start to finish before you follow the instructions and use it.

1. Listen carefully to your partner and notice how they express themselves. Do they predominantly use words to paint pictures? If so, their representational preference is probably visual. Do they enjoy talking, and playing or listening to music? If so, their representational preference is probably auditory. Do they use a lot of practical, concrete terms? If so, their representational preference is probably kinaesthetic.

2. Notice the direction in which people tend to look when searching their memory to answer questions. Visuals tend to look up, auditory to the side and kinaesthetic downwards. Watch for a while and look for an overall pattern.

3. When you have established their preferred mode of thinking, begin to move your own activities and use of language towards theirs:

   For Visual Partners
   • Use visual metaphors in your language.

- Show your love with acts of service and visible gifts, like flowers, paintings and written messages.
- Use your phone to send them lots of pictures and photos.
- Take them to the cinema and to beautiful places.

For Auditory Partners

- Use auditory metaphors in your language.
- Show your love by telling them what you love and appreciate about them meaningfully.
- Find out what sort of music they like, and find more of it.
- Take them to concerts.
- When you agree with them, don't just nod, but offer positive, verbal affirmation.

For Kinaesthetic Partners

- Use kinaesthetic metaphors in your language.
- Show your love by hugs and touches.
- Buy them presents that are rewarding to hold and to use.
- Take them to places where they can get a facial or a massage or enjoy physical activities like walking, dancing, tennis or sailing.

4. We all use all modes of thinking to some extent, so when you have an important message to convey, get maximum impact by including all three modes of communicating:

> Talk to the person in a *direct and meaningful tone*,
> *look them in the eye*, and
> *touch them in an appropriate way*.

5. If you are receiving an important emotional communication or a gift:

> *Hold* the gift or *touch* the person in an appropriate way,
> *look* at the gift carefully or *look* at the person as you
> *say* something thoughtful and appreciative.

YOUR ATTENTION IS POWERFUL

Your attention is a form of energy. At my seminars we show this with a very simple demonstration. I ask a volunteer to come up on stage and tell us what brought them to this seminar. My colleagues all pay close attention and listen carefully. After a minute or so, I interrupt and ask them to do it again. As soon as they start talking, I lean back and look away. I look for my phone or I beckon to a colleague or pick up a book. Hardly anyone can keep talking for more than twenty seconds. I'm not just being rude, I'm acting like the volunteer doesn't exist. All of them report that it makes them feel terrible. I always apologize afterwards, and I thank them for helping us do such a striking demonstration.

In everyday life the commonest example of this is a couple who spend a lot of time together, but both of them are always on the phone, on social media, messaging and browsing. I talked with a couple and the wife complained that her husband was never at home. He retorted he was there all evening, every evening, but her complaint was that his body was there but his attention was caught up in emails from work almost all the time. Even if someone is not reading an email or texting, phones can still limit communication. If you are with someone, whether child or adult, if their phone is on the table, the attention they give to you is reduced by the alerts on their phone and even by the *possibility* of alerts on their phone.

Your attention is one of the most powerful gifts you have. By paying attention to your partner you can:

- **demonstrate your respect**
- **understand them better**
- **notice small but important differences in what they say**
- **help them to discover more about themselves**
- **share deeper moments of intimacy**

The more you pay attention, the richer your relationship can become. I don't mean you should watch your partner all the time or stare at them all day. I mean that when they turn to you, give them your full attention.

When I am working with a psychotherapy client, I give them my full attention. I am not just looking at how they are and how they respond to me, I am always looking for the best version of them and that is the part I talk to and encourage.

How you pay attention is important

There are lots of ways of paying attention. The best way is to believe that the person you are talking to is important and valuable. Simon Cowell's father Eric used to say that everyone has a sign above their head saying, 'Make me feel important.'

It is easy to overlook how very powerful your attention is, especially if you think you are not in a powerful position. But your attention is *always* powerful. In this era of social media and global fame it is far too easy to imagine that a face-to-face meeting is not very important. If you believe that, it becomes a self-fulfilling prophecy. However, when you remember how powerful your attention is, you can transform all your relationships.

Attention and flirting

People flirt in order to attract the person they desire. When a relationship is starting both partners flirt and respond by paying attention to the other. This sort of attention is very arousing and rewarding because the sexual response is hard-wired into all of us. It is a very powerful force to make your relationship stronger and closer, and it is the ultimate creative energy.

Good sex brings people together and one of the best ways to make it better is to keep flirting, even long after you have agreed to be in a relationship. Flirting is a lot of fun in itself and it leads to better sex, which is perhaps the nicest form of communication that there is.

SUMMARY

BREAKERS

- **Personal criticism**
- **Defensiveness**
- **Stonewalling**
- **Contempt**

MAKERS

- **Rapport**
- **Listening and paying attention**
- **Responding to bids**
- **Admiration and optimism**
- **The love strategy**

REVIEW: HOW AM I COMMUNICATING?

Now that you have read this chapter, I'd like you to ask the chapter question yourself. Take a little while to think back over the last few days and weeks in your own life or in your relationship and ask, 'How am I communicating?'

➤ **Notice the times when you did or experienced any of the breakers.**

- *How did you feel?*

- *What happened next?*
- *What would you do differently now?*

➤ **Notice the times when you did or experienced or would have used any of the makers.**

- *How did you feel?*
- *What happened next?*
- *How can you have more of this in the future?*

Thinking now of all your answers and the whole chapter, ask yourself again, 'How am I communicating?' and notice all the kind, useful, loving, rewarding ways you are already communicating, whether small or large, and acknowledge your own success.

Now, in the 21-day relationship enricher section at the end of this book, or on your phone or in your diary, or even in a notebook, make a note of one new way of communicating you would like to use, or use more of, in your relationship, and try to use it within the next twenty-four hours.

ACTION

.

Q2.
WHAT ARE YOU
DOING?

Q2. WHAT ARE YOU DOING?

Richard Branson has a simple method of making important decisions. He looks at the situation and assesses the upside and the downside. He ranks 0 as minimum and 10 as maximum. If the upside significantly outweighs the downside he knows he should go ahead. The same principle can be applied to dating. If you want to ask someone out on a date, there is an upside and a downside. The downside is that they could turn you down. That may cause you to feel bad for an hour or two, even a whole day. So that is bad, but not horrendous, so let's give it a 3 or even a 2. On the other hand, the upside is that he or she could say yes, in which case you could have a good evening, start a relationship, or even end up getting married, so that could be worth an 8 or a 9. Compare the two and you get 2/3 versus 8/9. In this situation, it is clearly worth asking for a date. Whenever your assessment gives you a very low downside and a very high upside, that is a signal to take strong and massive action.

I had a colleague once who always, without fail, had a date or a relationship. He dated way more women, and way more attractive women, than anyone else, although he wasn't especially good-looking or witty or famous or anything. I was intrigued and tried for months to find out what his secret was. Eventually I understood. His secret was that he was not frightened of rejection. He just asked out more women, and more attractive women, more often than anyone else. His approach was the same one summed up by Henry Ford many years ago: 'If you want to increase your success rate, you have to be prepared to increase your failure rate.'

Some of the best things in life happen unexpectedly, and often that includes getting into a relationship. Sometimes, a couple meet each other's gaze across a crowded room and immediately feel an electric connection. In that moment, their lives change. Those relationships do happen but they are not that common. People meet in shops and businesses, through friends, through sports and completely by chance. Many, many people meet at work, more and more meet via dating apps, and every day people meet when they weren't expecting to meet anyone. Some of the best relationships start when people are not looking for a partner.

Quite a few relationships begin as just a bit of fun and gradually grow as people discover they like each other and get on better and better. Sometimes both partners fall in love at the same time, sometimes one person falls in love instantly and woos the other until at last they see how that person is truly loveable. Of course, it doesn't always work. We have all experienced unrequited love at some point, but life carries on and energy keeps flowing and just when you least expect it another person comes into your life. There is no special place to go to find the person of your dreams. The simplest attitude is to be open to having new experiences and meeting new people every day.

Meeting

If you get interested in someone, you want them to like you. We all want potential partners to find us interesting, amusing and attractive. You can indeed be all of those things, and by the time you have finished this book you will have many, many ways not just to be interesting, amusing and attractive but even more importantly to be confident about it. However, the most attractive people are not necessarily the ones who are the most poised, the most beautiful, the most talented or wealthy.

I had a patient once who was very worried about a date she had coming up the next weekend. She desperately wanted to appear witty and sophisticated and interesting.

'OK,' I said. 'Go ahead and rehearse that in your imagination. Close your eyes, go into the future and imagine your date takes you to a stylish restaurant and both of you are witty and charming all evening.'

She did that and nodded and gave me a little smile.

'Do you think that went well?' I asked. 'Will he call you next week?'

'I hope so,' she said.

'OK,' I said, 'Now do all that again. Imagine the whole evening again from start to finish, but at some point I want you to imagine that one of you knocks over a glass of water, and see what happens.'

She closed her eyes as before and after a few moments she blushed and burst out laughing.

'What happened?' I asked.

'Well,' she said, 'I knocked over a glass and he caught it, but the water went all down his trousers. And the fuss and the embarrassment and joking about it sort of broke the ice.'

Her imagination had shown her that while beauty and talent are attractive, it is very often our mistakes and our vulnerability that bring us together. Two people trying to be wonderful can easily turn into a competition. Two people being honest can turn into genuine connection.

Nominalizations

When we say, 'I really want a relationship,' or 'I have a long-term relationship,' the words imply that 'a relationship' is some kind of 'thing'. Of course, a relationship is not a thing. It is a process, an ongoing happening, an interdependent system. The beauty of a relationship is that while it gives us the comfort and reassurance of the familiar, it is also in a state of flux, constantly offering us something new. The technical term for words that make a process sound like an object is 'nominalization'.

If I want to clarify a discussion in which there may be nominalizations, I use the 'wheelbarrow test'. If something is really a thing, you can put it in a wheelbarrow and take it away. If you can't put it in a wheelbarrow, maybe it is a nominalization. A football match is an event, a process that lasts ninety minutes. You can't put it in a wheelbarrow.

The problem with making a 'relationship' sound like a thing is that the language implies that the relationship just is a particular way. It sounds as though it is stuck with particular qualities. We can talk about 'a good relationship' or 'a bad relationship'.

Saying 'a bad relationship' makes it sound as though it is a thing that is broken and can't be mended. But it is not made of concrete. Any word you use to describe it may be correct now or about some events in the past, but it does not have to be the way things happen in the future.

If we think about it, we all know this is true, but in everyday conversation, it is normal to use nominalizations. We have all had the experience of trying to discuss something and ending up in an argument we did not intend to have. Many times this happens because our ideas and discussions are inadvertently limited by the language we are using.

Here, for example, are three different ways to ask about a relationship. They are all asking the same thing, but the way they are phrased makes all the difference to how we are likely to answer them.

1. **How good is your relationship with your partner?**
   This question uses the nominalization 'relationship' and treats it like a fixed thing with specific qualities. It invites you to judge your relationship as one thing and give it marks out of ten. Once you have answered the question, it is like

you have summed up the relationship and that is just the way it is and it always will be.

2. **How do you get on with your partner?**

   This question points more towards the process of the relationship. It focuses on events and actions, and asks about what you are doing. Again, the answer will tend to sound like a judgement, but importantly it includes an element of action.

3. **Please tell me the story of your relationship with your partner.**

   This request is the one most likely to get an answer that includes all sorts of different events that have happened and does not necessarily sum up or judge your relationship. It treats your relationship as an ongoing process. The great thing about stories is that unexpected events happen. Furthermore, good stories often include difficult, dangerous or frightening events. This is the question that invites you to give the least judgemental and richest description of your relationship.

What you do

Relationships are processes. That means that your relationship is what you do. It is not what you dream, or wish for, or hope for, it is what actually happens. It is what you do. If you laugh together and play together that is what your relationship is. If you spend a lot of time talking about your relationship, then, for all that time, that is what your relationship is: it is a conversation about itself.

If a life is like a river, a relationship is a meeting of two rivers. Each life brings its own energy and currents and all the boats and flotsam that it is carrying. Each partner brings their own hopes and desires and ideas and imperfections and expectations and memories and fears and needs and emotional baggage and a whole inner world of imagination. You both bring so much to your relationship that you cannot possibly understand it all or sum it all up. Furthermore, none of us even know ourselves well enough to know what we bring. There is always more to discover.

Making an effort

A friend of mine was dating online. He is a nice guy, but he doesn't look like a model. One day he was delighted to be matched with a truly stunning woman who was keen to meet after they had exchanged just a few messages. They met at a pub in a fancy part of London and had a great time. He asked her if there was anything in his profile that caused her to agree to meet him.

'Yes,' she said, 'there was. You said you were into cycling and you had just bought an old bicycle for £5. I thought it was really cute that you obviously were not showing off.' What made him stand out and more attractive to her was the fact that he wasn't trying too hard to impress her.

On the other hand, one of the mistakes people make when they are in a relationship is that they don't try hard enough. When you really, really want a relationship, the best strategy is to not try too hard. When you have the relationship of your dreams and everything is perfect and you feel lighter than air, that's when you have to start working!

Being laid-back and relaxed may well get you a partner, but keeping him or her requires a bit of effort. Don't get me wrong – that effort is rewarded tenfold, but if you don't put it in, you don't get the reward.

In every relationship and every household there are chores to be done. People who don't pull their weight eventually generate resentment. At a deeper level, all those dreams and desires and fears and fantasies that you each brought with you will sooner or later turn up in your life together. When you make the effort to meet each other with positive energy and honesty, you get to know each other better and better.

Smallest thing

Throughout this book there are practical exercises with specific goals like improving communication or enriching your feelings of love, but very often I meet people who want things to be better but just don't know what to do or where to start. They feel stuck in a rut and seem to have forgotten all the things that brought them together in the first place. When I ask them what they want, it sounds as if they want a completely different life. They want to live in a different country, or have a different job, or want their partner to be twenty years younger. All of these changes seem far too big or downright impossible, so they just give up.

I remember one particular gentleman who told me that he hardly talked to his wife any more. All they ever talked to each other about were practical arrangements. In the morning, each of them read their own newspaper. In the evening, they watched television together in silence. They never touched each other. He wished it was different but he felt it was too late to change.

He was looking for a huge change to a very stable situation. So, I asked him to change his focus. I asked him to think of the smallest possible action he could do that would be the smallest actual movement towards the smallest possible improvement of the relationship.

I saw him a week later and he told me that one evening when he said good night to his wife, he touched her gently on the shoulder. He said that the next day it was as though the sun had come out from years behind the clouds. They had a little lightweight chat over breakfast, and as the days progressed, they even had a joke or two, until eventually, the atmosphere in the house was completely different. He felt relaxed and he didn't feel hopeless any more.

Everything we do in a relationship has meaning, and even the smallest things can have important meanings.

What is the smallest possible step I can take in the direction of a better relationship?

What happens next

As we explored earlier, a relationship is not a thing, it is a process. You can think of it as a story or a journey. Relationships often start with two people falling in love. When you are young enough and inexperienced enough you can think that 'being in love' is the reason and the goal of relationships. But actually 'being in love' is never more than part of the whole story. Falling in love and being in love happen to us. We don't choose them and we don't control them. They happen. Being in love is like a huge booster at the start of a relationship. The strength of a long-term relationship comes from our willingness to add loving to being in love.

Some people have a goal to get married. They feel that when they are married everything will be perfect. Marriage can certainly be a great thing. It is not for everyone, but for those who choose it, it is a commitment and a celebration and often a step towards starting or supporting a family. There are plenty of good reasons to get married. However, it is not a great goal for a relationship. A long-term relationship is a journey that may last as long as the rest of your life. Marriage is not a destination, it is more like a station on that journey. It is a big step, a brave, joyous, delightful step, but it is just another step on your journey together as a couple.

Jobs

Wherever you live, there are jobs to be done. The rent or the mortgage must be paid. Meals must be cooked, and cleaning and child care must be done. Money must be earned. If you live with your partner, you have to work out how you will share the tasks of the household.

Some people are very easy-going about it; others lay down a specific division of responsibilities. In the old days, social expectations were very strong, and very sexist. Nowadays, every couple has to negotiate their own deal. There is no Single Right Way. You have to find out what works for you. For some, bumbling along is fine. Other people negotiate and then re-negotiate regularly, so that both partners feel supported and respected.

Along with the tasks to be done, you may need to explore your perspectives on the relative importance of different jobs.

A friend of mine worked extremely hard to build up his business from nothing to a valuation of many millions of pounds. For a long time, he was flying round the world all week and would arrive home late on a Friday night exhausted. In the meantime his wife, who was also working, was cooking supper every night and making sure that their three children did their homework. In his work life he gets treated as someone of great importance and many people depend on him to live up to the responsibilities of leadership. But as he remarked to me, 'It is easy to imagine your time is more important or more valuable than your partner's.' He makes a point of cooking breakfast every Sunday. It is just one meal, but it helps him tune in to the family's values and priorities after a week in the grand but narrow world of business.

50/50

It is very difficult to compare the different tasks in a relationship. Is cooking more demanding than washing up? If you enjoy the cooking, does that mean that it counts for less? How can you measure emotional work? Some couples can discuss this sort of thing for ever without reaching a conclusion.

I have just one suggestion that I offer to couples who have this sort of disagreement.

It is inevitable that with two different points of view and the usual roller-coaster of ups and downs in a relationship, it will be impossible to ensure both parties are happy that they are each contributing exactly 50 per cent to the heavy-lifting part of the partnership. Therefore, I propose to them that they should both try to do more than 50 per cent of the jobs in the relationship. They don't try to make it equal. If both partners try to do more than their fair share, a lot of arguments simply disappear.

How much am I doing in this relationship?

Big and small

For some people romance means extravagance. They have fantasies about a weekend in Paris or floating through Venice in a gondola. They dream of visiting the Taj Mahal or holding their lover's hand as they sit at the top of a Mayan temple, watching the sun rise over the forest. If you are one of those lucky people for whom these fantasies come true, congratulations! If you are not, don't lose any sleep over it. Big moments like that can indeed be wonderful, but on their own they do not have a long-term effect on your relationship. If you want your relationship to last, to get better and to feel wonderful, what matters most is what you do every day. A cup of tea, a song, a flower, a joke or a kiss can bring a smile to your lover's face even on the most ordinary day. These things are so small and simple that we can easily overlook them, especially when life is stressful. But they can make a wonderful difference. We can all lift our moods everyday with very small, simple actions. Grand gestures are the icing on the cake, but the cake is the everyday relationship and that is where we can make the big wins.

Actions and words

A friend of mine was explaining to me that he couldn't really understand his new girlfriend and it was making him unhappy. She is a good-looking woman, a few years younger than him. He complained that she was a bit unreliable. She would stand him up on dates but then call the next day full of apologies. She said she wanted to be with him, but sometimes she would just disappear. She had cheated on him but, he explained, she told him over and over again that she loved him. They had lots of discussions, but he was still confused and unhappy.

I suggested that he do two things. Firstly, go back in his memory and review the last three weeks, to remember what happened and what she said and what he said and what he felt. He took a few moments to do that. He still looked confused and unhappy.

'Now,' I said, 'do it again. Review the whole of the last three weeks in your mind, but this time do it without the soundtrack. See it in your mind as a silent movie.' He did that, and gradually the confusion disappeared. It was replaced by sadness.

When he saw what his girlfriend was doing without

being confused by what she was saying, he could see their relationship more clearly. Her actions were not saying, 'I love you,' they were saying something more like, 'I like you a bit, and you are comfortable and helpful, but I am more interested in stuff that is happening somewhere else.'

That was not what he wanted to see. In fact, he so very much wanted to see something else that he couldn't see what was really happening. Both of them had been pretending to have a loving relationship. My friend is very kind and also very wealthy, but he was lonely. He was looking for love, but he allowed himself to be distracted by the intermittent attention of a good-looking woman. Her real interests lay elsewhere but she allowed herself to be distracted by the advantages of a wealthy admirer. I'm not making any moral judgement. People can make any sort of arrangement that suits them. But in this case, my friend was not admitting to himself what was really happening. He was trying to find a way to make it fit the fantasy in his head, but he could not do it. The best he could achieve was a certain confusion. In truth he had not found love. He needed to keep looking.

GETTING CLARITY

If you are confused and frustrated in your relationship, go through your memories and find the times when you were most confused and frustrated. It could be just one incident, or it could be lots of them. You can do this exercise as many times as you want until you get the clarity you need. Please read the exercise through from start to finish before doing it.

1. Choose one incident where you were confused and frustrated and replay it in your mind from start to finish. Imagine there is a screen in front of you and you are watching and listening to a video that someone has made of your life. Watch what happened and hear who said what.

2. Now replay exactly the same incidents but with the sound turned off. You can't hear any words that anyone is saying, you can just see what they are doing. Look at those two people on the screen and pay attention to the behaviour.

3. Notice how it feels as you watch the actions without words.

4. Now, acting as if you didn't know anything other than what you can see, make a commentary explaining as simply as possible what the people appear to be doing.

5. Now decide what advice you would give yourself in this situation.

6. Follow your own advice.

TRYING NOT TO DO THINGS

Every now and then someone tells me about their troubles and it is clear that they are trying their best but they aren't getting the results they desire. Over and over again, I have found that troubles arise when someone has an overwhelming desire *not* to do something. For example, one man told me his dad was always so angry that he lived his whole childhood in fear. He was totally determined not to be like him. He vowed never to lose his temper, but in his relationship he did so over and over again.

There are several problems with trying not to do something. First, your unconscious doesn't process negation in the same way as other thoughts. It has to go into the positive first and then in some way cancel it. If, for example, I ask you not to think of elephants, an image or idea of an elephant will flash across your mind before you can choose not to pay attention to it. Every time my patient thought 'I must not be angry', an idea, or image, or feeling of anger went through his mind. The more the unconscious held this repeated idea of anger, the more the anger built up.

Secondly, every emotion, even anger, has a rightful job. The purpose of anger is to let you know that one of your standards has been violated. Your anger is released in order to take action – for example, to defend yourself or the people, places or things you value. If you completely remove anger, you run the risk of loss or damage to the people, places or things that are dear to you. That will cause you suffering, and you may end up angry at yourself for failing to defend what you value, instead of using the anger to help you prevent the damage or loss.

Thirdly, it won't help if you just try to do the opposite all the time. If you decide, 'I will always be nice,' you will find yourself being nice when it is not really appropriate. You are only doing it to avoid ever being angry, but it might be the wrong thing to do. Always doing 'the opposite of anger' is as limiting as 'never doing anger'.

Fourthly, none of us can completely control our emotions all the time. Sooner or later, all the anger that has built up but not been expressed will spring out and it is most likely to do so when you are most stressed and least able to manage it well.

Finally, my client's desire did not lead him towards what he wanted to do. It just said, 'Don't get angry,' but did not help him decide what to do instead.

Rather than decide, 'I will not do what my father did,' it is more liberating, empowering and inspiring to ask, 'What would my father have done if he had focused exclusively on being the best possible example to his child?' The answer to that question is infinitely rich and will vary with every single context.

The languages of love

In his great book *The Five Love Languages*, Gary Chapman highlights how much we communicate to our partner by what we do. Chapman says that our actions are like a language, and some people prefer the language of action to any other. The best way to show our love to these people is through what he calls Acts of Service, which are actions focused on meeting the needs and desires of your partner.

Chapman is absolutely right to highlight actions and, as we saw in the previous chapter, we all do have certain preferences. It may be that people with a visual or kinaesthetic preference are particularly receptive to acts of service, but all of us can appreciate them. Furthermore, if we don't do anything at all, the relationship grinds to a halt.

Chapman is really just reminding us that in a relationship, one thing matters more than what we think about it, more than what we feel about it, more even than what we say about it.

What matters most is what we *do*.

A good story carries on

However good your relationship is now, it will change because time passes and time brings change. So you too must keep changing and continuing to nourish your relationship. A relationship is not a destination. It is not a single place where you settle down and live happily ever after. A relationship is a process. It is something you do every day.

Whatever you have been through, whatever lies in your past, whatever happened yesterday, it is possible right now to make your relationship more rewarding. Sometimes you have to make a special effort – release a belief that makes you feel like a victim, or makes you feel that you were unfairly treated. Remember your situation may not be your fault, but it is your responsibility. Often you will find that small efforts and gestures generate big rewards. As long as you and your partner are here, your story continues.

WHAT AM I DOING?

Too many people assume they know what the other person wants or likes. When we take the time to discover the wishes and desires we did not know, we make wonderful discoveries. If you have a sense that, however good or not so good your relationship is, it could in some way be better (and I think that covers all of us), this is the exercise for you.

1. Sit down together and take the time for both of you to ask and answer these three questions. When the other person is speaking, just listen. Don't discuss or dispute what they say at this point, and only ask questions to make sure you understand them.
   - *What do you need from me?*
   - *What am I doing that doesn't feel good to you?*
   - *What am I not yet giving you that would make you even happier?*

   Neither of you have to answer every question completely and perfectly, nor do you have to find the answers straightaway. It is not an exam or a test. It is a process of exploration so that both partners get a chance to express concerns and know that they are being heard.

2. If you feel confused or upset by what your partner says, wait and reflect for a while on what you have heard. In a little while, a few hours or few days, explore the ideas a bit further and, if necessary, negotiate a way to ensure that both of you increase your satisfaction.

SUMMARY

BREAKERS

- **Saying but not doing**
- **Trying too hard**
- **Trying too little**
- **Trying *not* to do things**

MAKERS

- **Doing your everyday tasks with love**
- **Taking responsibility for your actions**
- **Doing at least one observable action to add joy to your relationship every day**

REVIEW: WHAT AM I DOING?

Now that you have read this chapter, I'd like you to ask the chapter question yourself. Take a little while to think back over the last few days and weeks in your own life or in your relationship and ask, 'What am I doing?'

➤ **Notice the times when you did or experienced any of the breakers.**

- *How did you feel?*
- *What happened next?*
- *What would you do differently now?*

➤ **Notice the times when you did or experienced or would have used any of the makers.**

- *How did you feel?*
- *What happened next?*
- *How can you have more of this in the future?*

Now, thinking of all of your answers and the whole chapter, ask yourself again, 'What am I doing?' and notice all the useful, loving, rewarding things you are doing already, whether small or large, and acknowledge your own success.

Now, in the 21-day relationship enricher section at the end of this book, or on your phone or in your diary, or even in a notebook, make a note of one thing you would like to do, or do more of, in your relationship, and try to do it within the next twenty-four hours.

SELF-CARE

·

Q3.
HOW DO YOU LOOK AFTER YOURSELF?

Q3. HOW DO YOU LOOK AFTER YOURSELF?

A few years ago a very large piece of research with a sample of 24,000 people showed that the married people were, on average, happier than the non-married people. That sounds like a great advert for marriage, but in fact that was not the final conclusion.

The research was longitudinal. That means it wasn't a one-off survey but it followed the same people over a period of many years. The researchers looked back at the data about the happily married people in the years before they got married. They discovered that those people were also happier than other people before they were married. The revised conclusion was therefore quite different. The data shows that people who are happy before marriage are most likely to be happy when they are married. In other words, already being happy in yourself is the best predictor of a happy marriage.

This is one of my favourite pieces of research because it supports one of the most important truths about relationships: the strongest base for a good relationship is when both partners are happy in themselves. In this chapter we focus on how you can be happy in yourself, and how that makes it easier to get into a relationship and how it makes the relationship you are in more and more satisfying.

Safety briefing

Before you take off in an aeroplane you always hear the safety briefing.

'In the event of a sudden loss of pressure, oxygen masks will drop from the panel above your head. Pull the mask towards you and place it firmly over your nose and mouth. Secure the elastic band behind your head and breathe normally. If you are travelling with children fit your own mask first before assisting others.'

In other words, make sure you are safe before trying to help anyone else. You are no use to your own children if you pass out from lack of oxygen while fiddling with the elastic band trying to fit their masks. The same point applies to relationships. If you want the best for your partner, you need to look after yourself first.

I make a similar point at my weight-loss seminars. At my seminars, mothers will tell me they just can't find the time to take care of themselves. They will say something like, 'I have three kids to feed, a house to run and my husband needs x, y and z. I don't have time to think about my own food. I just grab what I can, whenever I can.'

My reply goes like this:

'Well, I think your kids and your husband should be very grateful for all the work you are doing for them. But they will be less grateful if you end up sick because you didn't look after yourself. Your kids need you to be alive and healthy.

That is more important than whether or not they have to wait another twenty minutes for their supper. The best way to look after them properly is to look after yourself. The more you neglect your own needs, the greater the danger of problems in the future.'

It is far too easy to forget about our own needs. Some people even get so confused that they think it is better to put themselves last. They imagine it shows true love if they always put their partner or children first. That is sentimental. It may even be romantic. But it is not true love. True love means that you must take care of yourself so you can take care of others to the best of your ability.

You make me happy

Sometimes I talk to single people who tell me that what will make them happy is a relationship. They really want a partner and sincerely believe that they will be happier when they find one. It is a common and understandable aspiration, but it is a bit misleading. The issue of happiness is one of the biggest sources of confusion in romantic relationships. A loving, kind, beautiful partner does make people happy. I would go further and say that sharing your life with a loving partner can make almost every part of your life better than when you were on your own.

However, the fact that a partner makes you feel happy

does not mean that a partner is *necessary* to make you happy, nor that a partner is *obliged* to make you happy. Actually, a far better way to put it is that having a partner can make you *more* happy, provided you know how to be happy in the first place. We are focusing on exactly that in this chapter.

If someone is unhappy and expects their partner to make them happy, they will sooner or later be disappointed. Of course, if there was a button to press marked 'Happy' we would all press it. Unfortunately, human beings don't work that way. Your partner can be loving and compassionate and a good listener, but he or she cannot 'make' you happy.

We all have some reasons to be unhappy, but ultimately happiness is the choice we make to let go of all of those reasons and to take up the chance to be happy. That is the best thing you can do for your partner: make yourself happy and share it with them.

Trying too hard

I was recently talking to a young woman who kept having rows with her girlfriend. She complained that she spent all her time trying to please her partner, which frustrated her because she never knew what she really wanted. She felt her girlfriend wasn't expressing her own real desires.

We have to trust our partners to find their own paths to happiness. Equally we have to give each other space to find our own paths. If one person tries too hard to 'make' the other happy, they are very likely to cause the opposite result. The other person may see them as needy or desperate, both of which are a terrible turn-off. More often, it just causes resentment and misunderstanding because something about the effort is wrong – it might be the timing, the pressure, or a million other things.

How do I make myself happy?

So, how do we go about making ourselves happy? Life itself is such an amazing miracle that happiness is the most natural response to being alive. It is true that a number of people have chemical imbalances which predispose them to a less happy point of view, but even though the cause may be chemical, these imbalances can be treated psychologically. For all of us, there is a risk that our natural happiness gets blocked by attachments to ideas and resentments. We can miss the beauty of what is actually happening if we are too narrowly focused on wanting our own particular version of reality. As Richard Bandler says, 'Disappointment requires adequate planning.'

There are external difficulties in life which can make us unhappy, but by far the biggest causes of unhappiness in relationships happen in our minds. When we make the right changes on the inside, everything on the outside gets easier and easier.

The audio trance in this system will allow your unconscious mind to systematically review your automatic beliefs and set you up to take advantage of every opportunity for happiness. The happier you are in yourself, the more you are able to enjoy your relationship, and the more positive energy you make available to your partner.

HAPPINESS IS AN INSIDE JOB

My good friend Dr Robert Holden came across a fascinating scientific study in which a thousand people were asked, 'If nothing in your life changed, could you still be happier?' Ninety-five per cent of the people said, 'Yes.' In other words, happiness is an inside job. Whatever is happening on the outside, what matters for happiness are the choices you make on the inside. We all know what it is like to feel stuck in a situation we don't like. People have difficulties such as jobs they're fed up with, partners who get grumpy, debts to pay or difficult neighbours. Sometimes, with enough time, we can change these things, sometimes we can't. However, we always have a choice. In fact, we are always making choices, whether or not we notice it. We choose to sit or stand, to make a cup of tea or to carry on working. Right now, you are choosing to continue to read this book, or to put it down at the end of this sentence.

Whenever we have feelings, and whatever feelings we have, we always have a choice about how we *respond* to those feelings.

Happy people typically make two choices. The first is, when there are events that are enjoyable, they choose to enjoy them. That seems so obvious, it sounds absurd that anyone would not do it. Unfortunately, some people get caught up in stress or negativity and they don't let themselves enjoy what they could. For example, I talked to a woman who had been away for the weekend with her boyfriend and told me it had been terrible. I asked her what happened. They had stayed at a luxury hotel by the beach, the food was great and they were there with a large group of people they knew and liked.

'So, what went wrong?' I asked her.

She felt that her boyfriend didn't pay her enough attention.

'Was he ignoring you?' I asked.

She told me that he would come and find her from time to time, ask if she was OK, and ask her to go and dance. She didn't want to dance so she said no and he would go away again.

So he didn't ignore her, but she felt too put out to accept his invitation to dance. She resented the fact that he wasn't attentive enough. She got stuck in her resentment, and she did not choose to let herself be happy.

The second choice that happy people make is that when things are difficult, they choose to understand them in terms of a positive frame. A difficult task at work, for example, is framed as 'a chance to prove my competence' or a broken leg is framed as 'a reminder of how grateful I am for the times when my body works well'. The young woman above was using the frame 'a weekend away with my boyfriend' and it made her feel neglected. If she chose to frame it as 'a weekend away with our friends' she would be happier that her boyfriend was happy and take the opportunity to enjoy time with those friends too.

We say that 'happiness is an inside job' because we can

always find a way to respond to our own situation and our own feelings that lead us towards happiness. As the philosopher Syd Banks used to say, 'You are only ever one thought away from being happy.'

Self-image

When you fall in love, your partner is the most adorable person in the world. When you get together with your beloved you should be the happiest person in the world, shouldn't you? Well, yes and no. It all depends on how you feel about yourself.

If you feel good about yourself, you can welcome your good fortune and enjoy it. However, people who feel bad about themselves will get stressed. They worry that they are not good enough for their partner and that can start a whole train of complications.

The man who most successfully addressed this problem was not originally a psychologist. He was a cosmetic plastic surgeon called Maxwell Maltz. He became famous in the 1960s by writing an excellent book called *Psycho-Cybernetics*. Dr Maltz found that most of the time when he performed plastic surgery on a patient, they subsequently had a significant rise in self-esteem. However, for some patients, it didn't matter how dramatic the surgery was, they still felt bad about themselves, and some would feel better only temporarily and then want more surgery. Maxwell Maltz concluded these people were 'scarred on the inside'. He would then teach them a simple self-hypnosis technique to improve what is referred to as their 'self-image'. This system uses my enhanced version of the original, powerful way to enhance your self-image.

We refer to our self-image when we think about ourselves and make decisions. Self-image creates a template of what we think we can achieve. If someone thinks, 'I'm shy so can't talk to people,' it becomes a self-fulfilling prophecy. All the limitations arise from that version of the self-image as shy. It is vital to have a self-image which reflects the very best version of ourselves.

Self-image in relationships

Interestingly, we can have different images of ourselves in different contexts. It is common to have, for example, a very strong, confident self-image in business but a much less confident sense of self in the field of romance.

Sometimes, a person can project all the beauty and attractiveness and desirability on to their beloved but then feel their lover is so wonderful that they themselves cannot measure up. They worry that if their lover discovers who they 'really' are, they will be disappointed. Therefore, they continually hide their true selves and try to appear 'better'.

This never works in the long-term, because when we hide our true selves, we prevent true intimacy. We need a good enough self-image so that we dare to be true to ourselves. The technique that follows makes sure you have it.

Looking good

Just before we get to that technique, there is one more myth to dispel. Millions of people spend billions of pounds making themselves look beautiful. Good looks are very highly valued in our society, and almost all of us have wished at one point that we were more beautiful. Surely life would be easy if we were super good-looking! Once again, it all depends.

When I moved to New York in the nineties I met many beautiful models. After a while, I noticed something peculiar. All these gorgeous models had boyfriends who treated them badly. This was down to two issues.

First, most men were so overwhelmed by the women's good looks that they became tongue-tied and self-conscious. One of the most unfair things that is said about good-looking people is that they are shallow airheads. That may be true of some people. However, there is a far more embarrassing truth: good looks bring out the shallowness in *other people*. Many people lose their cool when they meet people they find super attractive. Instinctively the models were looking for someone strong, someone who could stand up to them, who had enough self-confidence to make up their own mind. Unfortunately, they mostly got men whose confidence was built on self-obsession rather than self-awareness. These men treated them badly, most often because they were too insensitive and too unkind to do otherwise.

Secondly, models are continually hit on because they look good, not because of their character. It is difficult to find someone who sees you as an interesting person when everyone is mesmerized by your body. Their good looks can get them a partner, but they get in the way of people really getting to know them.

I have met many powerful celebrities who can confidently address audiences of millions on TV but who feel weak in the field of relationships. I've worked with highly successful business men and women who run global companies who don't know how to approach someone they fancy, or feel stuck and helpless when talking to their partner.

They need to transfer the confidence they have in the field of business or entertainment into their love lives. That doesn't mean acting like a diva or running a relationship like a business, it means bringing across the sense of competence and self-worth that helps them to relax, enjoy and engage fully in their relationship. I created the following techniques to help them, and they may well help you too.

THE EYES OF LOVE and THE ULTIMATE YOU

This is my approach to improving self-image. This is influenced both by Dr Maltz and the famous family therapist Virginia Satir. No matter how well you think of yourself, try these two techniques to make yourself feel even better. Please read them through from start to finish before you do them. Take a break of at least five minutes between them, to allow your mind to absorb the power of The Eyes of Love before you move on to The Ultimate You.

Practise both these techniques every day for a week, and thereafter use either or both of them whenever your self-image needs a boost.

 I have made audio tracks to guide you through these techniques. Download them at **www.paulmckenna.com/downloads**

THE EYES OF LOVE

1. Close your eyes and think of someone who loves or deeply appreciates you. Remember how they look, and imagine they are standing in front of you now.

2. In your imagination, gently step out of your body and into the body of the person who loves you. See through their eyes, hear through their ears, and feel the love and good feelings they have as you look at you. Really notice in detail what it is that they love and appreciate about you. Recognize and

acknowledge those amazing qualities that perhaps you hadn't appreciated about yourself until now.

3. Step back into your own body and take a few moments to enjoy those good feelings of being loved and appreciated exactly as you are.

THE ULTIMATE YOU

1. Imagine there is a cinema screen in front of you and now, on that screen, watch a movie of the ultimate you. See yourself doing all the things that you do or would like to do really, really well.

2. Watch that movie of you working, socializing, handling challenging situations or difficult people really well. Watch the way you stand and smile with natural authentic confidence.

3. Now watch yourself approaching and talking to the most attractive people you can imagine. Enjoy watching a movie of you talking to famous people and feeling as comfortable and relaxed as you do with your very best friends. See yourself cool and happy and having a great time.

4. Now when that movie looks really great and you feel really good about yourself in that movie, float over and into the you in the movie, see through the eyes of your ultimate self, hear through the ears and feel how good you feel living life like this.

SELF-SABOTAGE

If you suffer from self-sabotage, this is for you. Relationships require more than confidence. They require a deep level of trust. My own experience is a good example of this. I dated many women but I did not seem to be able to make a relationship last. As this pattern emerged, I developed two unhelpful beliefs. In the first, I saw myself as a victim of a pattern: I could not stop choosing the wrong women. In the second, I believed I could not stop myself from sabotaging my own happiness. My unconscious mind knew that I had been hurt in the past and it manufactured disagreements so that we would split up before it became too painful.

The unconscious mind is not logical but it is purposeful. I didn't say to myself, 'There's an unsuitable woman, I must chase her!' It just happened over and over again that I found myself being attracted to women and then soon afterwards breaking up with them.

The driver was in my unconsciousness. I had a deep unconscious belief that I was damaged and therefore condemned to be a victim. Furthermore, I had been hurt before so my unconscious was protecting me from more hurt by preventing me from letting anyone get too close. In fact, I didn't realize what was happening until after I had stopped, and that came about by using the next technique and also, as we shall see later, because of some work I did with my great friend Dr Ronald Ruden.

One day I was due to appear on morning TV and I was chatting to two women who were appearing with me. One of them, an attractive woman, was telling the other about how she kept sabotaging her own relationships. She kept picking the wrong guys and making the same mistakes, again and again. She turned to me and said, 'I don't suppose you could do anything about that?'

Well, the least I could do was try.

We got to work there and then and at the end she looked a bit different to me, sort of lighter and happier. She said she felt really good and thanked me very sincerely. It just so happened that she stayed in touch through a mutual acquaintance and I heard that within a few months she had met someone new and was in love. A few months later, she was married and soon after that they had a child. Her whole life changed in less than twenty minutes.

I hypnotised her and gave her the same suggestions that I have included in the hypnotic trance which accompanies this book. I also took her through Dr Richard Bandler's technique for defeating self-sabotage. I have written out the technique on the following pages.

DEFEATING SELF-SABOTAGE

Please read the technique* all the way through before you use it.

 I have made an audio track to guide you through this. Download it at
www.paulmckenna.com/downloads

1. Identify the two conflicting beliefs or positions within your mind. For example, part of you wants a relationship, but another part of you might want to stop you having a relationship because it believes that that will keep you safe. If that part is scared you will fail and feel upset, it may sabotage your attempts now and get it over with and minimize the pain.

2. Place your hands out in front of you, palms up. Imagine the part that wants to have a rewarding relationship in your right hand and the 'sabotage' part in your left.

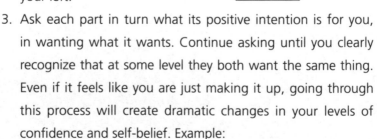

REWARDING RELATIONSHIP   SABOTAGE

3. Ask each part in turn what its positive intention is for you, in wanting what it wants. Continue asking until you clearly recognize that at some level they both want the same thing. Even if it feels like you are just making it up, going through this process will create dramatic changes in your levels of confidence and self-belief. Example:

- Relationship = experience love = have a partner = have a fulfilling life = SUCCESS!
- Sabotage = prevent closeness = prevent pain = safety = SUCCESS!

4. Imagine a new, 'super part' in between your hands with the combined resources of both your relationship and the sabotaging part. So, for example, can you have a relationship in a way that makes you feel safe?

5. Moving only as fast as each part can keep its positive intention, bring your hands together until the two separate parts become one with the super part.

6. Bring your hands into your chest and take the new integrated image inside you.

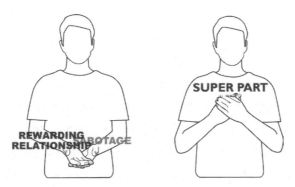

As you practise this technique, you will find it becomes easier and easier to resolve every internal conflict in this way, and when all the parts of yourself are aligned and moving in the same direction, you will have become focused like a laser beam on whatever you decide to do!

* This technique is used with the written permission of Dr Richard Bandler.

HAVENING

Havening therapy was created by my friend Ronald Ruden MD. Ph.D. Scientific studies have shown that it is amazingly effective at relieving sadness and reducing stress, trauma and psychological blocks, even if we don't know what the block is. Sometimes people know they feel blocked in an area of their lives, such as relationships.

Dr Ruden's work has been hailed as a remarkable breakthrough. He discovered that patterns of repeated touch to parts of the body combined with specific eye movements and visualizations have a rapid, reliable and predictable effect on our feelings. His years of research have created a significant advance in what is known as psychosensory therapy. The patterns of touch used in Havening are what enable a mother to comfort her baby and they are hard-wired into every infant. Havening combines these deep-rooted patterns of reassurance with sequences to break down the associations that triggered unhappy or uncomfortable feelings. As a result, in just a few minutes, we can now reduce the intensity of an emotion or feeling of unhappiness and establish calm.

This technique is not merely a distraction. Studies have shown that when we use the Havening technique, we reduce stress chemicals in our body and produce states of relaxation and calm. We also change the way our brain processes thoughts and feelings. The effect of the specific sequence I will share with you is to reset the way that your brain interprets and responds to stress. Over time, this actually alters the neural pathways in your brain.

I have included a Havening exercise in several of my books because it is such a quick and powerful way to heal our inner wounds. In learning about Havening, and in due course teaching it, I have done a great deal of Havening myself. I have also used it with many friends and colleagues. Dr Ruden and I discovered that Havening can even remove blocks of which we are not aware.

After I had been using Havening for a few years, I looked around the circle of my friends, acquaintances and colleagues and I noticed something remarkable. Everyone who had done a serious amount of Havening had changed or significantly improved their relationships. Those people who had tried to have relationships and kept failing had suddenly succeeded. This was true *whatever the presenting problem was for which they were using Havening.*

The removal of traumatic responses from deep memories by Havening appeared to have the side-effect of making people more capable of genuine, honest, enduring relationships. I had not realized that as I did more and more Havening, I began a journey beyond pleasure-seeking towards the happiness of a long-term relationship.

Releasing blocks

Initially I had no idea that Havening would have this side-effect, but it intrigues me. It implies that when people are not upset or blocked, they naturally gravitate towards long-term intimate relationships. It was after an intense amount of Havening that things started to change for me. It was halfway through the process, when I was wondering if it was ever going to work, that suddenly it shifted and I felt a profound feeling of relief.

Later I began to explore the use of Havening specifically with people who felt unable to form relationships. Time and time again, I found the following sequence of events played out.

A person would tell me they couldn't do relationships, or they never worked out. When I asked what was stopping them, they could not tell me. If I asked, 'Is there a block?', they would say yes, and if asked them to visualize it, every one of them was able to do so. They saw something like a black mountain, a heavy cloud or a huge grey wall. I would ask them to focus on that image as we did the Havening and, over and over again, the image would fade away and disappear.

Follow-up reports revealed that their capacity for relationships had improved. This is not yet a formal, scientific study but these anecdotal reports are so compelling that I wanted to share them with you straightaway. What struck me as so powerful was that the individuals did not need to know the details of the 'block' in order to remove it.

Havening is far from the only element that matters, but it forms a central part of the system in this book. If you too want to get off the merry-go-round of trial and error and broken relationships, it is a basic building block of something more long-lasting. The most wonderful part of it is that it can heal wounds of which we are not even aware. With Havening, you don't need to know what caused the belief that is holding you back. You can dissolve it at the unconscious level. Maybe I had the belief that 'love equals pain'. Maybe I had a belief that I was not worthy of love. We don't need to spend years in analysis to find out what went wrong. With Havening, you can simply dissolve the blocks and restore your natural confidence and loveability.

A SAFE HAVEN

Please read through the following exercise before you do it. You should practise this sequence of eye movements, body touches and visualizations several times until you know it off by heart. Then you will be able to use it any time you need to get rid of unhappy feelings and swiftly feel calm and relaxed.

 I have made a video to guide you personally through Havening. Download it at **www.paulmckenna.com/downloads**

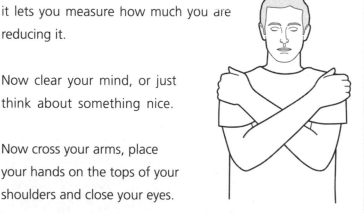

1. Pay attention to the discomfort or the block you wish to remove and notice what it looks like in your imagination. Now, rate its strength on a scale of 1 to 10, where 10 is the most powerful and 1 is the smallest. This is important as it lets you measure how much you are reducing it.

2. Now clear your mind, or just think about something nice.

3. Now cross your arms, place your hands on the tops of your shoulders and close your eyes.

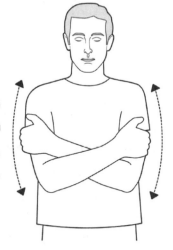

4. Now stroke your hands down the sides of your arms from your shoulders to your elbows, down and up, again and again.

5. As you carry on stroking the sides of your arms, imagine you are walking on a beautiful beach. With each footstep in the sand, count out loud from 1 to 20.

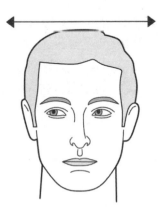

6. Now, keep your head still while you keep stroking your arms and move your eyes laterally to the left and to the right.

7. Still stroking the sides of your arms, imagine walking down a flight of stairs and count out loud with each footstep.

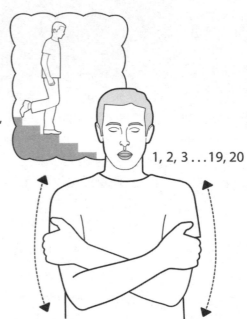

1, 2, 3 ... 19, 20

8. Now open your eyes and check, on your scale from 1 to 10, the number of the feeling now. If it is way down the bottom of the scale, congratulations – you have personally changed your own feeling state. If you think that the unhappy feeling is not yet reduced enough, just repeat the Havening sequence until it is reduced as far as you want.

Many people experience remarkable positive changes immediately after a Havening session. However, even if you are one of those people, I recommend you do this Havening exercise every day for at least 21 days.

PRACTICAL SELF-CARE

When you have used these techniques, you will have reset your self-image and removed the discomfort created by unconscious blocks. Now you are well placed to make positive, practical changes. You have a proper sense of your own worth, so it is time to check that you are respecting it. Don't forget that some of the most important things in our lives are simple, everyday events.

MEET YOUR OWN NEEDS

Every human has needs. To survive we need food, shelter and rest, but to have a fulfilling life we need a lot more than that. We need company and privacy, we need intimacy and respect, we need beauty and resilience. We all have to meet as many of our needs as we can.

ASK FOR WHAT YOU WANT

To meet some of our needs, we need other people. Privacy, intimacy, sex, friendship and support are all needs we meet through others. The questions and techniques in this chapter, and throughout the book, will help you to get your needs met. You may not always have them met by the first person you ask, but you can keep asking until you find the people who are willing to meet your needs.

QUALITY TIME

We all need quality time with our partners. It is very easy to fill our diaries with business and family needs. Now you know that it is important to put yourself and your partner in the diary too! Whether it is a date night, or just a couple of hours where the two of you can talk and relax together without children, mobiles or TV, you now know you need to make that time. If you are one of those people who needs time on their own, make sure you take that time too.

Surround yourself with the right people

We have friends we choose and we have acquaintances who happen to us. Every year or two I clear out my address book. I scroll through the names and I ask myself a simple question.

'Who takes my energy up and who takes it down?'

The answers are instantaneous. There are some people who are energy-drainers. They are like vampires or what the Chinese call 'hungry ghosts'. They always want something, whether it is attention or time or money or help or answers, but whatever you give them it is never enough. Such people are drawn to criticism, they hunt out negative interpretations, they are pessimistic and they bring me down, so I delete their numbers. Misery loves company but I don't want to be around that kind of company.

The right people to have around are kind, positive and

lucky. A study of lucky people found that a key element of their makeup was simply that they believed themselves to be lucky. The more they believed it, the more their luck increased. In the trance, we will specifically boost this element of your unconscious self-image.

As you use the exercises and techniques in this book you will make the changes that attract more of the right people into your life and, equally importantly, it will help you bring out the best in your partner and other people around you. You can start a virtuous circle of making each other shine and feel better and better.

Boundaries

Psychology and psychotherapy have created a whole dictionary's worth of new words and new meanings to analyse our daily life, and many of them are not really necessary. However, there is one word I have found really helpful and that is 'boundaries'. In a psychological sense 'having good boundaries' means having a clear distinction between what belongs to you and what belongs to other people. This is not about ownership of objects but about responsibilities and feelings. For example, good boundaries help to keep private conversations private. People with poor boundaries are willing to gossip about things that were said to them in confidence.

If two of your colleagues are having a disagreement at work, having good boundaries will help you to avoid getting dragged into it. If your partner has a disagreement with his or her family, or children, or ex, or boss, then having good boundaries means that it is his or her business and you only need to be involved insofar as it affects your relationship.

I like to visualize boundaries like that white-picket fence around the garden of an all-American home. What is inside the fence is mine, what is outside is not. Good boundaries stop other people interfering in your private business and they stop you getting pulled into other people's business.

Boundaries do more than protect you. They also create a private space into which you can invite your partner. When you have good boundaries, you will not overshare inappropriately with people. When you both have good boundaries, it allows you and your partner to share your intimate feelings in safety.

What is really happening

When you are honest and realistic with yourself about your needs, you are in a good position to be honest about your desires and what your partner really wants. One of the biggest challenges in relationships is when there is a big difference between what the two partners really want.

Some people enjoy having a companion, they enjoy sex,

they like to hang out and have fun and share beds and meals and housing and holidays, but they aren't thinking, "This is it! I totally want to be with this person for ever!' They are busy enjoying their lives right now and they are not making plans for the future.

Other people want to enjoy life now but they also have plans. Maybe they want monogamy, maybe they want children, maybe they want to get married.

Many problems arise simply because people are unwilling to admit to themselves or their partners what they really want, *even when they know the answer.*

The difficulty is multiplied because some people avoid these questions and some people lie. Some people don't want commitment but do want sex, so they pretend they are open to the idea of commitment.

Other people very much want commitment but pretend they are happy with just having sex when that is actually not enough for them.

However, when you have removed the unconscious blocks and you know yourself better, you will become very aware if there are times when you are letting wishful thinking blind you to what is really happening.

When we are honest with ourselves, we stop trying to persuade ourselves that reality is the way we want it to be and we pay attention to what is actually happening.

When you know how to meet your own needs, when you know you are more than good enough, when you have the resilience and strength to be honest with yourself, then you are strong enough to say goodbye to someone who is not heading in the same direction as you. If you want children and they don't, if they love getting drunk or high and you don't, if their religion is more important to them than your love, then I believe it is OK to leave and find someone who shares your desires and values.

Ongoing

We all love to be cherished, to feel wanted and even needed, but when need turns to neediness, everyone turns off. Whether or not you are in a relationship right now, whether you are starting a new one or whether you have been with your partner for twenty years, an important part of what you contribute to every relationship every day is your willingness to look after yourself properly. Just as neediness is a real turn-off, so self-care is a real turn-on.

The techniques in this chapter reinforce the foundations of self-care and the whole system will make it stronger than ever before.

SUMMARY

BREAKERS

- Waiting for my partner to make me happy
- Self-sabotage
- Stopping your appreciation of life

MAKERS

- Give time and energy to looking after yourself every day
- Build and sustain a positive self-image
- Maintain good boundaries
- Havening

REVIEW: HOW AM I LOOKING AFTER MYSELF?

Now that you have read this chapter, I'd like you to ask the chapter question yourself. Take a little while to think back over the last few days and weeks in your own life or in your relationship and ask, 'How am I looking after myself?'

➤ **Notice the times when you did or experienced any of the breakers.**

- *How did you feel?*
- *What happened next?*
- *What would you do differently now?*

➤ **Notice the times when you did or experienced or would have used any of the makers.**

- *How did you feel?*
- *What happened next?*
- *How can you have more of this in the future?*

Thinking now of all your answers and the whole chapter, ask yourself again, 'How am I looking after myself?' and notice all the kind, sensible things you are already doing, whether small or large, and acknowledge your own success.

Now, in the 21-day relationship enricher section at the end of this book, or on your phone or in your diary, or even in a notebook, make a note of one new way in which you would like to look after yourself, and try to do it within the next twenty-four hours.

GENEROSITY

•

Q4.
WHAT ARE
YOU GIVING?

Q4. WHAT ARE YOU GIVING?

Most love songs are about the beginning of love, and some are about the end. There are not so many songs about being happily married or doing the school run because it doesn't seem so exciting. Songs work better when they are about yearning or loss.

Love songs are about how much the singer loves and desires the man or woman they fancy. They are all about yearning and flirting and desiring and seducing, or losing, missing and regret. They sing about wanting a person, their love, the beauty and their body.

Looking for love

When we are looking for love, we are scanning the world for a person who attracts us. We are driven by our desire. We are focused on the things we hope to possess. We are looking for the joys of seduction, of flirting and making love. We want someone beautiful and sensitive, someone with a good sense of humour and a sense of adventure in bed.

We can all dream about a lover, even when there is no prospective lover in sight, and we all have a mental shopping list of the qualities we believe would be most wonderful and romantic. Every dating site profile has a list of qualities; what we are looking for and what we are like.

'I want a guy/woman who is taller/shorter than me.'

'She/he must look hot.'

'He/she must be politically aware/creative/rich/ spiritual.'

'She/he must love dogs, gardening or extreme sports.'

Some qualities are widely attractive, like money, fame and beauty. Other qualities are simply a matter of personal taste. For example, some people really like redheads, others are not bothered either way. For some people, fashion and looking good are all important; others don't care about that but value intelligence and intellectual achievement above all.

Whatever the details, at the start of a relationship we are focused on what we want. We seek gratification.

Instinct

We are drawn to our partners by two different forces. The first is instinct. Sex is the basic, hard-wired instinct that prevents the human race from dying out. The attraction between men and women flows in and around us all the time. It provides a little electricity when we are socializing, and giving and receiving appreciation is part of the pleasure of socializing.

The strength of our desires and of other people's attractiveness varies over time, but we tend to go for the same types. Even though we talk about fancying someone or looking for a partner as though we are making choices, a good deal of our sexual behaviour actually happens instinctively. We experience it, just as we experience hunger for food. There are some kinds of people we find attractive and others we don't; it is just a matter of sexual chemistry. We can see that some people are very beautiful, yet we don't find them sexy. Others are not so obviously beautiful, yet very attractive indeed. We all simply have our own preferences.

Our instincts don't just push us to have sex. We also seek partnership and security. There are biological reasons for this as well as social imprinting. Women who get pregnant will be better off if they have a partner who is willing and able to help them with the challenge of having and raising a child. Men who become fathers have an incentive to stay with the mother to protect the children who carry their genes and ensure they survive and prosper. These instincts are always at work. They don't completely control us, but they always exert their influence.

Unconscious connection

The second force that brings couples together is more mysterious but it has fascinated humans since ancient times. Plato tells us of the myth that originally human beings had four legs, four arms and two heads. These beings were too powerful, so the god Zeus cut them in two, making the men and women we are today. As a result, we are all seeking our 'other half' from which we were severed. You are looking for somebody who 'completes you'.

This idea was explained in more psychological terms in the last century by the famous psychoanalyst Carl Jung. He proposed that in our unconscious each of us has a part which is the opposite gender from ourselves. So, men have a female part in the unconscious that he calls 'the anima', and women have a male part in the unconscious that he calls 'the animus'.

Jung says that when you fall in love, you project on to your beloved your 'animus' (if you are a woman) or your 'anima' (if you are a man). When we fall in love, we may know very, very little about our beloved. You could meet someone for five minutes and fall immediately in love. You know almost nothing about them, but your anima or animus 'fills in the gaps'. You can imagine sharing your deepest thoughts, you can imagine looking into their eyes and feeling a rich and deep connection, you could even imagine playing with the children you have together. This sounds a bit fantastic when written down in black and white like that, but it is far more common than we admit to our everyday, rational selves. All these details and this wonderful imagery comes from the anima or the animus.

The downside of these unconscious parts is that they are not developed or educated like the conscious self and they can overwhelm our own behaviour as well as our perception of our beloved. When they do that, they tend to express all the more selfish and wilful attributes of the opposite gender. That is why lovers' arguments can be so trivial and yet so heated at the same time. They appear far more childish and difficult than the normal everyday self, because when the anima or animus take over, we are being more childish and difficult than normal.

Ideals

Nowadays, although relationships are not constrained by traditional gender roles, these archetypal patterns are still in play all around us. In Jung's thinking the anima and animus are complex concepts – they are both idealized and problematic. For each of us, the anima or animus is shaped by social expectations, by our own experience of the other sex and also by human limitations and failings. However, we don't need to go into all the complex details to understand relationships better.

These ideas explain why we idealize our lovers when we first meet them. It is quite natural and beautiful, and it releases the fabulous energy of 'being in love'. The ideal version of your lover is part of who they are, but it is not the whole of them. While we are in love, we have a golden opportunity to get to know the reality of our partner and the unknown parts of ourselves.

When you first fall in love, it can seem very simple and it can also be very selfish. We love the other person so much we want to see them, be with them and possess them as much as possible. That phase is delightful, but it is only the beginning. We cannot help but start by being idealistic and there is nothing wrong with that. What makes your relationship strong and lasting and truly rewarding is the next stage in which we get to know ourselves as much as the other. We discover our own weaknesses and vulnerabilities and those of our partner, and we learn to be kind, generous and compassionate. As we become more realistic, we become more adult and more genuinely loving. This is where the focus changes from getting what we desire to learning what we can give. We discover the rewards of giving to our partner as we find the relationship completes us both.

Both sides

When two people fall in love, they both initially see the wonderful, shiny, ideal version of the other. As the relationship continues, both of them see all the other parts too. All of us have wonderful and less wonderful aspects. The anima and the animus are the ideal version of the other, but they also include the most unconscious, undeveloped, selfish version too. If we match each other enough to fall in love, then our unconscious drives will relate both at the high level of love and the low level of defensiveness. This is why the person whom we deeply love is also the person who can 'press our buttons' and make us furious. As the English theatre critic Kenneth Tynan put it, 'We seek the teeth that made the wounds.'

Our partners trigger our most vulnerable emotions. That can be very, very annoying. The upside is that little by little we get to know our own sensitivities and can gradually learn to take control of behaviour that used to be driven completely outside of our awareness. We get to know ourselves better and better. We are no longer slaves to compulsive reactions. Often we discover that the qualities we find most annoying in others also exist in ourselves, but in a manner in which we could not recognize them. The faults and flaws that we saw in our partners are also present in us. The relationship becomes like a mirror, and as we discover more and more about ourselves, we become more free to act in accordance with our own true values. We can keep the positive elements of our ideas and learn to avoid being taken over by the childish parts of the animus or anima.

A journey

This psychological journey may sound complicated but it is simpler than it sounds. In the first phase of relationships we are delighted by our new partners. We love their eyes, their laughter and their smile. We find everything about them fascinating and wonderful. We feel lucky to find someone who understands us, someone who cares and someone who is so interesting. It is a delicious and lovely time, and we get all the joy we have been hoping and yearning for in our hearts.

The first rush of 'being in love' is like a free gift of energy and happiness. It is lovely, whatever you do. If you want a longer relationship and long-term happiness, however, you have to put in your own energy as well.

Sooner or later your lover will do something you don't understand, something unexpected or even something you don't like, and you begin the discovery of the rest of their character. Having been brought together by a magnetism that is quite beyond your control, you now start the business of learning to live with each other.

From getting to giving

You can still enjoy all the beauty and fun that you see in your partner, but now your relationship is asking you to give. As challenges show up, you have to give energy, attention and compassion and learn to live with stuff you don't understand yet.

Therefore, you have to look in two directions and keep asking yourself:

'Am I being loving and fair to my partner?'
and:
'Am I being loving and fair to myself?'

These questions don't have a single answer. You have to keep asking them and keep answering them every day. None of us are perfect, and we can easily veer towards being a bit selfish or giving too much. 'Too much' or 'too little' cannot be measured or prescribed in advance. We know what they are by what we feel.

Giving

There is a folk story of a man who dies and is taken to see both Heaven and Hell. Hell is a narrow room so long that he cannot see the end. Down the middle is a table and on either side are seated thousands of people. All of them have a plate of delicious food and each one has a spoon in their hand. But the handles of the spoons are so long that they cannot get the food into their mouths. The man is whisked away and taken to see Heaven. Heaven is a narrow room so long that he cannot see the end. Down the middle is a table and on either side are seated thousands of people. All of them have a plate of delicious food and each one has a spoon in their hand. The handles of the spoons are so long that each person is able to feed the person sitting opposite them on the other side of the table.

When we give something to others, we also bring happiness to ourselves. In part, this comes from the joy of seeing the happiness of those we love, and in part it comes from the satisfaction of having enough resources that we are able to share them with others. But even when we give away time, energy or things that we can ill afford, we can still feel good. Sometimes there is a sense of satisfaction of living up to our own moral codes. Other times it comes from the sense that we are able to repay to the world the favours we have received.

A few people seem to be immune from feeling the joy of giving, and these are often people who are happy without intimate relationships. They can enjoy companionship and sex but are not interested in intimacy. If you seek intimacy, you will have to seek it elsewhere. If you suspect you are such a person, then you will be most happy with someone similar.

Balance

It is fairly obvious that if one partner is very selfish the relationship will suffer. It is less obvious, but just as true, that if one partner gives too much, the relationship will also suffer. If you give your lover something and then feel resentful when you don't receive a gift in return, it shows you gave a bit more than you could afford emotionally. Maybe you wanted to be so close that you could give completely unconditionally, but your heart is telling you that you couldn't do it. It was your decision to give the gift, so you can't blame your partner. You just have to let that go, and then dial down your own generosity. You need to recognize your own automatic reactions and then choose more consciously what you will do. That takes a certain amount of energy, but it is always rewarded.

We all need to bring awareness and balance to our relationship, but with a spirit of generosity. It is not a matter of trying to find out exactly how much to give and exactly when to stop, but rather to pay attention to the feeling of balance, and make sure that one is not trying too hard and giving too much, nor being too possessive and not giving enough.

I knew a couple once who had very, very different incomes. One was a nurse and the other a chief executive. After a couple of dates, the nurse invited the chief executive to join her in her favourite activity, which was hiking. They went off to the hills and slept in a tent on the Saturday night. The following weekend he invited her to join him. He flew her in his own aeroplane to his country house. The relationship flourished because both of them were willing to give and to receive according to their personal values and wealth. He was happy to go hiking, so she was happy to go away in his plane. The key is not mathematics here but simply being absolutely honest with yourself, and then with your partner, about what you are truly willing and able to give and what you truly feel.

People don't always notice that their relationships are unbalanced, especially if they are getting what they like and their partner insists on giving to them. Sometimes people give more and more and more, in the hope that their partner will reciprocate. Maybe that happens sometimes. More often when I hear about it, the receiver just protests, 'But they insisted! They wanted to give me that time/attention/money/etc.' If one partner takes on the role of the long-suffering martyr who does all the housework, the other might notice and help, but they are just as likely to sit back and enjoy having all the work done for them.

If things are not going so well and you are feeling ripped off, you need to talk about it. If your partner doesn't know about your feelings, they may just carry on doing whatever they do. When you both share how you really feel, you can discuss how to make your generosity work better.

The purpose of talking and reviewing is not to get caught up in point-scoring but to find better ways to feel balanced in the relationship.

Practical giving

Generosity takes many more forms than giving actual physical objects as presents. There are gifts of action, practical help, indirect help and unseen assistance.

As Gary Chapman shows us in *The Five Love Languages*, actions which he calls 'acts of service' can be a language. To some people they are the most meaningful language of all.

Soon after I started dating the woman who became my wife, I was up early and I decided to make her a cup of tea and bring it to her in bed. Visual is her preferred form of thinking and representation, and I could see that, to her, bringing tea meant more than words. It was a visible, practical, unrequested action that showed her I care for her.

Even something as dull and domestic as taking out the rubbish can be an act of love. If one partner never cooks, they can easily overlook all the mess created in a kitchen. If they take the time to tidy up, bag up the recycling and take out the rubbish that practical action is an important form of giving. Sometimes your partner cares a lot about things that don't matter much to you. A simple way of giving is to care about those things as well.

Children create a lot of work. When they are young, they need attention all the time and they need their nappies changed. It is amazing that even in these liberated times many men don't seem to be around when a nappy needs changing. It's not actually a big deal and it is a fair bet that the mum is thinking that changing nappies is a job that should be shared by both parents.

Some people are perfectly happy to divide up the jobs in a relationship according to traditional gender roles, and there is nothing wrong with that if both parties agree. However, it is not a recipe for happiness to make assumptions about what your partner will or won't do. Nowadays, we are free to share jobs regardless of gender, so it is up to all of us to decide our own arrangements. If both parties can do more of what they like, then so much the better. If nobody likes doing the cleaning, then maybe you agree to share it equally. It doesn't matter what your grandmother did, or what your father thinks about it or what I think about it, or anyone else. In each relationship the parties have to work it out for themselves. Everyone has to agree how to split the jobs and, just as importantly, agree to renegotiate as time goes by and the situation changes, or you discover that some tasks are easier or more difficult than you anticipated.

Priorities and wishes change over time, so in every relationship the partners need to negotiate and renegotiate arrangements that offer them both the most joy and satisfaction. If you are confused about your own relationship, a good question to start exploring how to rearrange it is to ask, 'Is the relationship overall taking away energy or giving me energy?' If you feel you are giving more than you get back over the long term, it is time to renegotiate.

Psychological gifts

The greatest gifts we can give to our partner come from our behaviour. We could buy diamond rings or sports cars or exotic holidays but the joy of any gift, however extravagant, will evaporate quickly if we don't have a loving attitude. I have met too many wealthy men who imagined that a jet-set lifestyle was enough to ensure their wife's affection. One of the most important gifts we can give is time: paying attention, helping, listening and letting your partner do their own thing. We give the gift of attention when we make a point of complimenting new clothes or haircuts. One small compliment may not seem at all important, but it carries the meaning 'I am paying attention to you' and that is a very important meaning indeed. The smallest gift – a card, a cup of tea or a single flower – can melt your partner's heart and touch more deeply than the most expensive gift on the planet if the giving comes with true, loving generosity.

Many of our attitudes and behaviours are driven by the programmes or automatic habits in our minds. Almost all of us have outdated beliefs, assumptions and attachments which get in the way of being truly loving. The great benefit of a relationship is that it gives you a huge incentive to clear out all the programmes that are no longer helpful so that you can be properly generous and loving to your partner. When we have true inner confidence and are free from attachments, it is possible to contribute massively to the success of our relationships. Havening and the audio trance (see pages 118 and 26) will greatly boost your inner confidence.

We can be flexible about the means of reaching the successes we desire. We can be humble about our opinions, because being 'wrong' does not mean we are bad or lacking or personally failing. It just means we can learn more.

Plenty of people like to sound off down the pub about their other half or gossip to girlfriends about the shortcomings of their partner. The energy, concern and emotion that is expressed in that sort of unloading actually belongs inside the relationship because that is where it started and that is where it can be transformed into connection and intimacy. You could even say that misunderstanding and disagreement are the fuel for the relationship because they are the opportunities for growing together. In the next chapter, we will explore some amazing ways to move from arguments to intimacy.

Invisibility

All of us have had the experience from time to time of feeling that people don't notice what we have given them. You work hard, you plan, you give it reality and they totally miss it. It happens. Then you have to take a deep breath and decide. If you are hurt, you have to admit it – but without criticizing or blaming. Own your own disappointment, don't blame the other. Or you can just let it go. But *really* let it go. Don't let it fester and fester until you burst out in blaming and anger.

By the same token, we learn that we can't see everything that is making a relationship work. A lot of the most valued parts of a relationship are invisible. A few years ago, a businessman bought a large talent agency for twenty million pounds. His attitude was very practical. Cut out wasteful overheads and get more business in. He treated people like commodities he had bought. He treated them as pawns and didn't take into consideration their humanity and personal feelings. The agents felt increasingly neglected and badly treated. They tried to explain he wasn't making the most of the business but he didn't change his attitude, so the agents decided to leave and set up their own business. He didn't realize the power of relationships.

'You can't do that!' he protested. 'I have contracts with all the clients.'

'Oh, we will honour all the contracts,' the agents replied. 'You will get all the money you are owed. You just won't get any more. Despite your contracts, you don't own us. You don't own the relationships we have with our clients, the artists. All the new business will come to the new agency because our clients are moving with us.'

The businessman had bought a long-established, prestigious brand with hundreds of contacts, but eventually he had to cut his losses and sell the business for just two million pounds. He fundamentally misunderstood that personal relationships were the core of the business, and the true value of the agency was in the relationships that had been built on trust and consistency over time.

Giving up

When we build a relationship, we have to break down some of the habits, assumptions and behaviours that were part of our previous life. Not so much giving, as giving up.

Sometimes these are very little changes. For example, a friend of mine who had lived on his own for years got a girlfriend and soon she moved in with him. He had a habit of making himself breakfast, more or less on autopilot, while he woke up in the morning. It took him months to remember to ask his girlfriend if she too wanted breakfast at that time. He had to give up a useful, self-centred habit and create a new one that was similar but good for both of them, not just him.

SUMMARY

BREAKERS

- **Focus on getting**
- **Taking projections personally**
- **Controlling how a gift should be received**

MAKERS

- **Focus on giving**
- **Building balance**
- **Giving time and attention**

REVIEW: WHAT AM I GIVING?

Now that you have read this chapter, I'd like you to ask the chapter question yourself. Take a little while to think back over the last few days and weeks in your own life or in your relationship and ask, 'What am I giving?'

➤ **Notice the times when you did or experienced any of the breakers.**

- *How did you feel?*
- *What happened next?*
- *What would you do differently now?*

➤ **Notice the times when you did or experienced or
would have used any of the makers.**

- *How did you feel?*
- *What happened next?*
- *How can you have more of this in the future?*

Thinking now of all your answers and the whole chapter, ask
yourself again, 'What am I giving?' and notice all the kind,
generous gifts you are already giving, whether small or large, and
acknowledge your own success.

Now, in the 21-day relationship enricher section at the end
of this book, or on your phone or in your diary, or even in a
notebook, make a note of one new gift, of whatever nature, that
you would like to give, and try to do it, or start doing it, within the
next twenty-four hours.

DISAGREEMENT

•

Q5.
HOW DO YOU
DISAGREE?

Q.5 HOW DO YOU DISAGREE?

When you fall in love with someone wonderful it is hard to imagine disagreeing with them. It is easy to get on with people when we agree with them. Your beloved is so kind, so thoughtful, so clever and so on that disagreement could never happen. Until it does. The strength of a relationship is forged when we find out how to get on during disagreements with our partners. And sooner or later you will disagree with your partner.

It doesn't really matter what you disagree about, what matters is *how* you disagree. This chapter explores how you can turn the difficulties of disagreements into a source of creativity and intimacy.

Embracing conflict

One of the joys of a close relationship is the feeling that you are finally with someone who understands you. Naturally it is disappointing when you find yourself in conflict with your partner, but it is an inevitable part of a relationship. Nobody's perfect and, although we all like to imagine otherwise, you will both have different points of view. Sooner or later, you will see things differently in a way that you find frustrating or annoying. Those times are all opportunities for learning, although we don't necessarily feel that at the time.

Most of us don't like conflict, so often we try to avoid it and hope the issue just goes away. If it does, that's great. Maybe the issue wasn't that important after all. But if the issue doesn't go away, it rarely works to just keep avoiding it. We have to face it and go through it.

In the long term, this saves an awful lot of time and hassle. Perpetually avoiding disagreements gradually creates more and more distortions. A friend told me recently about meeting an old school friend, who, on parting, said, 'Don't tell my wife.' He had told her he was at work that day but in fact he just wanted to get out of the house for some peace and quiet. His wife thought she was the centre of the universe and would not tolerate disagreement. He wanted to get a cleaner, she wouldn't let a stranger in the house, so he ended up doing the cleaning. He wanted to visit his brother in the USA, she changed her mind and he had to cancel the trip. He had only three responses to his wife. He argued with her and would lose. Or he agreed with her when he did not want to and he felt bad. Or he would lie to her about what he was doing.

We could say that the relationship has problems because he is not looking after himself and his own needs (see Question Three). But equally we could say the problem comes because his wife insists on getting what she wants all the time and does not care for the needs of others. Or we could say that the problem is that they have not yet found a way to disagree properly and learn and grow from the experience. Sadly, it looks as though the only agreement that couple will make will be to go their separate ways. It is absolutely not necessary to break up a relationship just because you disagree about some things, but it is necessary to find out how to disagree constructively.

Disagreement is unavoidable in any relationship. The better you are able to do it, the more quickly you get the advantages of both points of view. Disagreement can be a creative process leading to new solutions and better understanding.

The magnetism of negativity

Disagreement is not always creative and useful. When you get into an argument and the adrenaline is flowing, there is a strong urge to keep going. When this combines with our pride, it feels like a very strong compulsion to argue more and more forcefully. We don't really choose to be over the top, but if we are overwhelmed by anger, the anger takes charge. I call this 'the magnetism of negativity'.

If you watch other people arguing you can often see how bizarre it looks, but it is difficult to see that from the inside. The anger reduces self-awareness, and angry people seem to want other people to get angry too. That is not a conscious desire. Another way to put it is that anger is infectious.

We have to use our awareness to avoid getting infected. This is a bit more difficult than it sounds because there is a weird attractiveness to anger. It is a bit like a form of intoxication. There is a high, and an appealing sense of being able to let rip with a righteous excuse. It takes some extra effort not to do that.

We can see this effect clearly when it is amplified by alcohol. Alcohol reduces inhibitions, so when people are drunk and angry they can get very out of control. They are full of remorse when they sober up. They didn't choose to be horrible, they just went along with the drink and the anger and then the anger and adrenaline took over.

All of the techniques in this book are effective alternatives to getting sucked into the magnetism of negativity and I ask you to practise them often so that if you are threatened by that magnetism you have a real, accessible, practical alternative.

Winning and losing

As I have built up my business, I have found it useful to convince people of my point of view. It is helpful to have a clear, single-minded vision and the persistence to make it happen, so I learned to win arguments in the business world. Personal, romantic relationships are different. It is not like running a business where keeping control is an important strategy. If I win an argument, that means someone else loses and, in general, it is not a good thing to be the cause of your partner losing. In relationships, I learned to let go of winning or losing. I might be right or my partner might be right, but the best outcome is not that one of us is right but that both of us have more understanding. When arguments arise, my goal is no longer to win, but to let the argument develop into a conversation which increases understanding.

Some arguments are emotional, others are practical, and sometimes they are both. In all cases, I have found that if I insist on getting my own way, I risk losing the nourishing connection of my relationship. So now, instead of thinking of disagreement as an argument I find it helpful to think of it as a discussion to work out how to meet a practical problem. The more I think of arguments like this, the fewer arguments I have.

In an intimate relationship, a good disagreement teaches us something. It is where your self-awareness and your closeness to your partner grows.

Honesty

I have found that it pays to be honest, especially about the things that are challenging or embarrassing. Generally speaking, the more challenging the subject, the greater the reward of honesty. However, honesty calls for tact. You may be honest about your point of view, but that doesn't mean your opinion is objective fact. When I have to say something difficult to a friend or colleague I always start with, 'I need to tell you something as a friend' to make it clear that my thoughts are a constructive form of criticism.

In relationships, it is helpful to meet three conditions if you have something honest to say which could be misunderstood.

- **First, choose a moment when you are both calm, relaxed and getting on well.**
- **Secondly, be tactful. Don't use rude words. If you can, use neutral words.**
- **Thirdly, take it one step at a time. If you have a lot to say, you don't have to say it all at once.**

If your partner puts on weight and you don't like it, you have to tell them. If your partner tells you they don't like the fact that *you* have put on weight, it pays to reply honestly. If you feel hurt, say so. If you feel ashamed, say so. If you want to lose weight but are frightened, say so. If you want their help, say so. If you want the other person to drink less alcohol, or lose weight as well, or come home earlier, say so. None of these conversations are easy and there is no 'right' answer to them, but as you have the conversation you share your honest feelings, and if you do that with kindness the solution that works for your relationship will emerge. The techniques that follow can help you to work through the issues that arise. That might take a little time, but it will lead to solutions.

Psychological understanding

The science of psychology has made amazing advances in the last few decades. We know so much more about how the brain works, how trauma is encoded and released, and the thousands of patterns of human influence. So now that we have access to all this new knowledge, we should be able to make relationships work better, shouldn't we? Well, it all depends on how you use the information. When you are in a relationship, everything you do has an effect on your partner. Even your attitude affects your partner. When you give someone a psychological label, you are behaving like a scientist and that makes the other person the object of a scientific analysis. It also means that you have stopped behaving like someone *in* a relationship and are behaving like someone outside observing the relationship.

If a person is labelled as, for example, a 'neurotic', that puts an unhelpful judgement on all of their behaviour. It is a limitation both for the person labelled and the labeller. That is completely different from the interactivity of an intimate relationship, and it stops both parties being emotionally open to each other.

Using psychological labels, even if in fact they are objectively right, does not help a relationship move forward. If you want to stay in the relationship, you need to stay with whatever feelings it brings up in you. When either party uses labels to limit or analyse the other person, that can easily be heard as a criticism, and it falls into the danger area identified by Dr Gottman (see Question One). If two people are disagreeing about a problem – say, when to visit the parents – then one calls the other 'passive aggressive', it doesn't help them move towards a solution. Instead it just creates another element of the argument. Now there is 'When to visit the parents', and also 'Am I passive aggressive?', plus possibly, 'Why did you call me that?'

The deeper problem with labels is that they imply a fixed state. 'Passive aggressive' describes a fixed type of person and doesn't give any indication of how to change that. 'I don't feel I know how to talk to you right now' describes a difficulty in an ongoing process. That is much easier to deal with than a label. Psychological labels can be helpful to professionals who need to make treatment decisions. They don't help to build intimacy in relationships.

Autopilot arguments

Some arguments seem to run themselves. They start with a really small difference of opinion about, for example, where to go for dinner or which film to watch, and a few minutes later there is a whirlwind of accusations and recriminations. 'Where did that come from?' you might find yourself asking.

Every case is unique in the detail, but there are several factors which contribute to the lightning-fast explosion of an argument from nowhere. The first and most obvious is that a disagreement in the relationship has been repressed somewhere else. For example, Catherine was jealous of the attention her partner Bill paid to another woman in the pub. She suppressed her anger and it came out sideways when she exploded at him later for forgetting to buy milk at the supermarket.

It's not about the milk, so Bill can't understand why she is so upset. His natural response is defensiveness. He is likely to retaliate with a criticism. Both parties are now riled up and go on the attack. Associative thinking helps them recall past incidents where the other party was at fault. This is when phrases like, 'And another thing . . .' get used. Defence and attack both release more and more adrenaline and that leads easily to both parties being taken over by the 'fight' part of the 'fight or flight' instinct.

These factors – repression, defensiveness, associative thinking, adrenaline and the fight or flight response – can all be unleashed in less than a minute and both parties get swept up into an argument that nobody wants and is far more painful and damaging than they intended.

But it doesn't always happen. How come some people can just have a laugh about a flash of aggression and other people get swept up into a full-on row? If you are relaxed and confident in yourself, you can hear a criticism as a potentially useful piece of information without feeling any personal attack at all. You know that either the other person misunderstood you, or you have made an error that could be corrected. So, if you are in a good mood, you won't take it personally.

What is it really about?

In the previous example, Bill was unaware that Catherine was jealous. There may be several reasons why Catherine is upset and one event triggers her resentment about several issues. Equally, as Bill defends himself by attacking, he activates in himself resentments that were buried but unresolved. So, an argument can very swiftly become a magnet for many other issues. If either of them manages to pause, they can then explore the primary cause of the upset. It's generally helpful to avoid making assumptions and to remain curious.

Maybe the argument is about actions, or maybe it is more about meaning. Maybe the other person feels overlooked or forgotten and wants some reassurance. And very often we don't know ourselves how we got into an argument. When the emotion takes over, we quickly get lost.

Clearing automatic defensiveness

Perhaps you have been in the same situation as I have, when I felt I was in good humour and a minute or so later, completely unintentionally, was arguing as if my life depended on it. My defensive reaction felt completely automatic, and in a sense it was. Reactions like that arise from the unconscious mind. My unconscious mind felt threatened and triggered my defensiveness. It was not a deliberate, conscious decision at all. It may be that as a child my needs were ignored, or my voice was not heard, or I was blamed for something that was not my fault. I do know that by using Havening (page 118) to clear the trauma at the unconscious level, I have reduced my tendency to be over-defensive by healing the inner wounds that used to be so upsetting. Nevertheless, the old habitual behaviour may still be triggered, even though much less powerfully.

When defensive habits are triggered, all you need to do is notice it and pause. That is much easier said than done. Luckily, there is an amazing technique which helps to centre and relax us instantly in the face of stress.

From head to heart

The Institute of HeartMath was set up in the early 1990s to study the role of the physical heart in health and well-being. Their work and its applications have become so successful that their stress-management programmes have been taken up around the world, including by all four branches of the US military.

They discovered that actively focusing on the physical heart measurably reduced the presence of stress hormones, increased anti-ageing hormone levels, and enabled peak performance in a variety of situations.

They have developed a number of tools for increasing the coherence between the electromagnetic signals of the heart-brain and the head-brain, and they are all built around one basic idea: when you shift your attention from your head to your heart, your body relaxes, your mind gets clearer, and your brain releases the positive chemical changes of natural relaxation.

You can use the following technique any time you are experiencing stress in your body or your mind. It will help you to feel better almost immediately, usually in less than a minute. In addition, you may get insights into what to do to make things more the way you want them.

HEARTMATH

Read through this technique several times and go through the motions even if right now you are not feeling stressed at all. Practise the whole sequence as many times as you wish until you know you have memorized it well enough that it is almost automatic when you need to use it.

 I have made an audio track to guide you through this. Download it at **www.paulmckenna.com/downloads**

1. Become aware that you are experiencing a stressful feeling in your body or that your mind is racing.

2. Put your hand on your heart and focus your energy into this area. Take at least three slow and gentle breaths into your heart, maintaining your focus on the feeling of your hand in the centre of your chest.

3. Now, recall a time when you felt really, really good – a time you felt love, joy or real happiness! Return to that memory as if you are back there again right now. See what you saw, hear what you heard, and feel how good you felt.

4. As you feel this good feeling in your body, imagine your heart could speak to you. Ask your heart how you could take better care of yourself in this moment and in this situation.

5. Listen to what your heart says in answer to your question and act on it as soon as you can.

You can use HeartMath to stop yourself reacting automatically. You don't try to fight against your reaction, you just pause for a moment, and in that time the reaction itself easily and naturally evolves. Your unconscious is no longer automatically defensive, so it relaxes and you are free to bring a more relaxed awareness to the situation.

CONFLICT RESOLUTION

You can prevent automatic defensiveness by using HeartMath, but there may still be issues about which you and your partner disagree and they need to be sorted out. I have personally been inspired by the work of Marshall Rosenberg,* who invented a process to deal with conflict which he calls Non-violent Communication. In the 1960s, Rosenberg was involved in mediation between rioting students and college administrators, and in work to ensure peaceful transition to integrated schooling in areas that had long been segregated by race. His work was much appreciated and word spread so far that eventually he ended up training people in sixty different countries.

All humans need food, warmth and shelter, but Rosenberg realized that we have many other needs, such as those for love, intimacy, self-respect, leisure, privacy and so on. We are all seeking to get our needs met. Rosenberg suggests that we can reduce conflict by looking past criticism and judgement and focusing on our needs or the needs that others are seeking to have met.

* To find out more about Rosenberg's work visit: www.cnvc.org

CONFLICT RESOLUTION

Rosenberg's process for conflict resolution has four steps. If we substitute it for our usual styles of argument, conflict can disappear. Rosenberg suggests we keep each of the following steps separate and take them in order.

1. Say what you observe

State what you observe as objectively as possible and avoid being critical or judgemental. This sounds simple but it takes practice because many common words have criticism built into them. For example, 'When I hear you speaking' is neutral. It is not judgemental. However, 'When you criticize me' is itself a critical way of describing the speech. The trick is to find a neutral description.

In our earlier example, Bill could respond to Catherine by saying, 'I can hear you're upset.'

If you find it difficult to find a neutral description, you could explain that's the case, and apologize that your words may not be the most eloquent but you will do your best.

2. Say what you feel

We all need to recognize that our emotions are not controlled by other people. For example, when I say, 'I feel fearful', I am taking responsibility for my own emotions. If I said, 'You make me scared', I would imply you are responsible for my emotions. That would not be helpful because it could be heard as blaming you. No one else can control your feelings. Feelings arise within you, and you have a choice about how you respond to them.

Bill could say to Catherine, 'I'm shocked! I feel really uncomfortable about this whole thing!' He is not blaming Catherine for how he feels, but honestly reporting his own experience.

3. State your needs

Every feeling has an underlying need. If the need is met, I feel better. If the need is not met, the feeling is prompting me to create a strategy to get that need met. Bill could say, 'I need to feel understood!'

4. Make your request

Bill feels really confused, but doesn't know why, so instead of reacting defensively, he could say, 'I need to understand exactly what's upsetting you, so we can stop it happening again.' If Catherine can tell him about her need for security and affection, they will soon find common ground.

This sequence helps you to identify your unmet needs and to express them clearly to your partner, and he/she can do the same.

When the unmet needs have been identified, you can both work towards meeting them and move on. If your partner can't meet those needs, you both now know what your needs are and you can search for other ways to get those needs met.

In the examples above, Bill's words might sound a bit clunky.

That is fine really, because we are not trying to set up a pattern that sounds easy. Instead, we are interrupting the highly energized but destructive progress of an argument. You will feel pretty good about sounding clunky when it causes arguments to vanish.

Please practise this sequence every day for a week so that you can remember it when you most need it in the heat of the moment. The more you practise it, the easier it is to remember. Even the most trivial disagreement is good enough to practise this. You can even make a game out of it with your partner. The more you both get used to the sequence, the easier it will be to use when you really need it.

Even with the smallest difference of opinion, run through this sequence with each other:

1. *Say what you observe.*
2. *Say what you feel.*
3. *State your needs.*
4. *Make your request.*

Listening

If both partners are up for it, Rosenberg's process is a fabulous way to resolve conflicts. However, sometimes people just won't want to do it. They would rather keep arguing than be clear about their needs. If you are confronted with that, you can still listen to them using Rosenberg's basic approach of avoiding criticism and judgement. When you listen like this, you filter out all the judgemental words and phrases, and focus on the feelings and the true needs being expressed behind their words.

When it is your turn to speak, you can check your understanding with the other person by saying, for example, 'When I listen to you, it seems to me that you have a need for some attention and respect from me. Does that sound right to you?'

In this way you can build agreement, one step at a time. Remember sounding clunky is well worth it if it builds agreement and understanding.

Are you having the same argument over and over again?

Every long-term relationship is a journey of discovery. There are ups and downs, and sometimes it feels like two steps forward and one step back, but the process carries on and gradually we learn more and more. Unfortunately, it isn't always like that. A very common problem in relationships is that the couple have the same argument over and over again.

If both parties are good-humoured about it, they may just accept that it is an issue that will continue to provoke them. Other couples learn, eventually, to avoid or bypass the situations that provoke that argument. Some people, however, get tired of it, and they need to sort it out.

In my experience, every argument like this is sustained by one painful, difficult and challenging issue that is never mentioned. In Marshall Rosenberg's terms, there is an Unmet Need. When people have the same argument over and over again, there is usually an issue about an unmet need of one or both parties that they are ashamed of, embarrassed about or unwilling to mention for some reason.

MOVING THE ARGUMENT ON

Read through this sequence of steps several times so that you can remember it. If you can't remember it when you need it, come and find this book. That will also give you a useful break in an argument!

Step One

Recognize and acknowledge with your partner that this argument is very similar to many previous arguments and ask your partner to pause with you in the middle of the argument.

Step Two

Suggest that somewhere in the relationship there is some uncomfortable fact, thought or element which you are both avoiding mentioning.

Step Three

Suggest that behind this painful fact, thought or element there is an unmet need.

Step Four

Invite your partner to speak and then listen to them without interrupting, commenting or judging.

Step Five

Acknowledge whatever comes up. If something is said that opens the discussion towards a solution, keep talking. If nothing comes up, use this idea to brainstorm between you:

'If we were to talk about this next week and we were able to take one real, observable step towards solving this conflict, what would have to be different about our talk next week?'

Step Six

Be patient. Let Step Five carry on for as long or as short as the energy of the conversation allows and then let it go.

What are you arguing for?

It takes a fair bit of practice to pause at the very moment an argument is about to kick off. However, as you practise, you become better at it, so when you are able to do so, you are free to ask yourself lots of helpful questions. You can use Marshall Rosenberg's technique to resolve the conflict. You can also learn a bit about yourself. I once asked myself a question which was extremely revealing. I was in the middle of an argument and, as I heard myself and the other person going at it, I suddenly asked myself:

'What am I really arguing for?'

What, in other words, was my purpose? That question led to a cascade of other questions. Did I just want to win? If so, why? What was so important about winning? Did I have a real purpose or was I just taken over by a defensive reaction? Did I want to convince my opponent that my view of the world was superior to theirs? Did I want someone to change their behaviour? Did I, deep down, really want a happy life? Did I want to enjoy myself?

I realized that whatever I wanted, arguing was not the most efficient way to get it. Arguing is not persuasive. Often it just antagonizes people. Persuasion is much, much stronger than argument.

Over time, whenever I have paused when an argument was about to kick off, I have found many different answers to that question:

'What are you arguing for?'

The single most common experience I have had is that at the precise moment I want to argue, I have a strong feeling that the topic is very important to me and I must fight for it. However, if I pause and ask myself that question and a little time passes, I notice that the sense of urgency and insistence lessens. I see, very often, that now it is less important than I thought. Later still, I have often found that by letting go of the argument, other possibilities have arisen and everything turns out fine in a way I had not expected.

On other occasions, I still feel the need to make my point, but I can do so with less heat and we reach agreement more easily than we would have achieved by argument.

Secondary gains

Some people like to argue. They enjoy the drama and energy of conflict, the cycle of accusing, arguing and making up afterwards. They do not want solutions. They are not arguing because they want a particular outcome, but because they want the argument. The argument gets them attention and keeps people engaged and aroused and focused on them. Psychologists call this sort of indirect benefit a 'secondary gain'. In other words, they are not arguing to win the argument, they are arguing because they get something out of arguing.

If you have tried to stop an argument a couple of times and it doesn't work, it is well worth asking yourself, 'Is my partner getting something just from arguing?'

If you suspect the answer is yes, the follow-up question is, 'What secondary gain are they getting, and is there a better way for them to get it?'

Sometimes the secondary gain is of deep and significant importance; at other times, it is not. It may just be like children play-fighting. They are not really fighting to win but to play, to tease and have the fun of rough and tumble. I have a friend who is always late. He sometimes gives you a reason, sometimes he doesn't. I think the real reason he does it is for secondary gain. It is his way of saying, 'I'm important.'

Secondary gains can be both conscious and unconscious. Some people quite consciously stir up trouble because they want the attention it gets them. Other times the secondary gain can be quite unconscious. I worked with a very talented man who repeatedly made a mess of his career just at the point that he was about to be massively successful. Using hypnosis to regress him, we discovered an incident in his youth when he'd told his mother, 'I'm going to be super-successful!'

His mother had replied, 'Oh, you don't want to do that. Those successful people all die of heart attacks!'

The unconscious mind is highly purposeful but not logical, so from that moment it had protected him from heart attacks by making him sabotage his own success.

There are many situations that are driven by secondary

gains. For example, you might be puzzled because your partner seems to keep changing their mind. 'Yesterday they wanted X, today they want Y. I don't know what they want!'

Well, maybe the answer is hiding right there under your nose. Maybe what they really want is *to keep changing their mind*! It is not as energetic as arguing but it is another form of getting attention. Similarly, some people encourage flirtation not to begin a relationship but simply to enjoy the attention of someone else flirting with them. They don't want the relationship at all, but they do want the attention. They may or may not be conscious of what they are doing, and it doesn't matter whether they are or not. If you do want a relationship and you don't want to give your attention to someone who does not want to go any further, the wise step is just to move on.

In the trance section of this system, we will go through a procedure which clears out dysfunctional and counterproductive patterns yet continues to ensure that your unconscious mind protects you.

Patience

Some of the most confusing arguments happen when the people involved have completely different motivations. For example, one person may be logical and the other may be focused on emotions. The emotional one tries to make an emotional connection. The logical one tries to clarify the issues. To the emotional one, the attempts at logic feel like the other person is avoiding the importance of the emotions. To the logical one, all the expressions of the emotion appear illogical and unhelpful.

I have found it helps to step back and see the big picture, the whole of your life together and all the good things that you know you have had and will have in the future. That puts this particular difficulty in the context of a loving and fulfilling relationship. Sometimes the best solution is not to seek a solution. Just let the other person say their piece and then stand back and wait.

You can agree that nothing is solved and the argument is not finished but you don't have to carry on arguing right now. You can agree to discuss it again later. As time passes, both of you will be in a different state of mind and you will see things differently. Alternatively, you may just decide to use the idea below.

A great way to stop an argument

I have left one of the most powerful responses to near the end because it is a brilliant way to deal with disagreements you have not been able to overcome any other way. It is short, it is simple and sometimes this is all you need:

Agree to disagree.

I used to think that in an argument you just kept going until one of you won or someone gave up. It is astonishingly liberating to realize that it is not always possible to reach agreement. I am grateful to my wife who introduced me to this very powerful solution. People have different points of view and sometimes all we need to do is to accept that.

Negotiate

Sometimes it is OK to agree to disagree about your opinions, but if it is a decision about a practical matter, you may need to reach an agreement. In that case, you have to negotiate. Some people believe the best deal is when they have won as much as possible and the other party has lost. That is rarely the best way to do business and it is certainly not the best way to negotiate in your private life. I prefer to think about negotiation as a conversation that keeps going until both sides are happy with the outcome.

If you want something and your partner is not happy about it, you have to find a way to make it acceptable or offer something else they do want in return. So, for example, if you want to go off fishing for the weekend and leave your partner to look after the kids, you could start by offering to do the same for your partner – look after the kids while they have a weekend off. You don't have to offer the same thing, just something else they feel happy to accept as equivalent.

It may not seem loving or romantic or sexy to talk about negotiation, but it really is worth doing because the sign of a good negotiation is that both are happy with their side of the bargain. If you try too hard to be nice or loving or generous and pretend to be happy when you are not, sooner or later the resentment will surface. It is far better to stand up for what you want and keep negotiating till you are satisfied. When you are both happy with the deal you are getting, love flows more easily.

There are whole books written about negotiation that are worth reading, but here are some basic guidelines:

- **Be clear about your aims but flexible about how you get there.**
- **Whenever you agree to something that is a cost, ensure you receive in return something that is a benefit.**
- **Don't give a long list of reasons why the other person should agree with you. Give them one reason. Keep your other reasons to use one at a time to respond to their objections.**
- **Don't be distracted by critical comments or fall into an argument. Focus on the practical elements and remember you are trying to reach an agreement.**
- **Get as much as you can of what you want, but make sure the other party gets enough benefits to make it worth their while to stick to the agreement.**

Solutions

Every relationship is different and they can all evolve over time so there is no single protocol for dealing with all arguments. My good friend, life coach Michael Neill, says there are three factors that sustain a healthy relationship: (1) be kind, (2) enjoy each other, and (3) don't take it personally. 'Don't take it personally' means that whatever people say, you can accept that as what they want to say **without taking offence**. This is another way of expressing John Gottman's idea of avoiding personal criticism and Marshall Rosenberg's idea of seeing past personal criticism and looking for the unmet needs.

Most arguments are not logical activities. Logic is great for scientists, philosophers and mathematicians but relationships are about *relating* and that as an emotional process. Feelings are why we are in relationships, so nine times out of ten, feelings really do matter more than logic. That's why being good-humoured is so useful. Being cheerful, kind and optimistic helps you to see the light side of things and positive alternatives to problems. That is why kindness is one of Michael's three factors. It can seem strange to remind ourselves to be kind to our partners when the feelings that draw us together seem to be way more powerful than kindness, but kindness is a good basic attitude to maintain when troubles and arguments press upon us.

SUMMARY

BREAKERS

- **Automatic defensiveness**
- **Labelling**
- **Secondary gains**

MAKERS

- **HeartMath**
- **Conflict resolution**
- **Agree to disagree**

REVIEW: HOW DO I DISAGREE?

Now that you have read this chapter, I'd like you to ask the chapter question yourself. Take a little while to think back over the last few days and weeks in your own life or in your relationship and ask, 'How do I disagree?'

➤ **Notice the times when you did or experienced any of the breakers.**

- *How did you feel?*
- *What happened next?*
- *What would you do differently now?*

➤ **Notice the times when you did or experienced or would have used any of the makers.**

- *How did you feel?*
- *What happened next?*
- *How can you have more of this in the future?*

Thinking now of all your answers and the whole chapter, ask yourself again, 'How do I disagree?' and notice all the useful, loving, helpful things you are doing already, whether small or large, and acknowledge your own success.

Now, in the 21-day relationship enricher section at the end of this book, or on your phone or in your diary, or even in a notebook, make a note of one technique you want to use, or would like to bear in mind next time you find yourself in a disagreement, and look at that note every day so that next time it happens, you remember to call upon it.

LEARNING

•

Q6.
WHAT ARE YOU LEARNING?

Q6. WHAT ARE YOU LEARNING?

The answer to this question is the most personal part of this system. We all have challenges to face and opportunities to learn, but for each of us the lessons to learn are specific to the unique challenges of our own history. When we choose an intimate relationship, we have an opportunity to learn about our partners, and about life. It is also a special opportunity to learn more about ourselves.

We fall in love in our heads

When you fall in love, it usually goes like this. You meet someone and they catch your eye. There is something about them that makes you look twice. They are attractive to you. You talk a bit and introduce yourselves, and that feels good. Later on, you think about them. You go home and you find yourself planning to meet them again. You imagine hanging out with them. In your mind you represent them in the same vivid, warm way that you think of other people who are dear to you. You imagine all sorts of activities and conversations and you just can't stop thinking about them. You talk to your friends and this new person keeps turning up in your conversation. You've fallen in love.

When we are in love, everything about our lover seems wonderful. A new partner brings a new world view and enriches our lives. If your new partner is into something you thought was dull as ditch water, their interest suddenly makes it seem remarkably fascinating and desirable. You may take up new sports, read new authors and find new heroes.

Mixed up with all they bring are the ideas and fantasies we project on to them, and sometimes our ideas are very different from the real nature of our new lover, so we can have many surprises as we discover, little by little, how they really live, feel and think. On the other hand, sometimes our projections work like a magical invitation, and the new partner enjoys living up to the expectations we create.

There is a popular metaphor about getting to know people which says it is like peeling off layer after layer of an onion. You think you know them, then you discover there is another layer to peel off, then another, and so on. The metaphor is vivid and it makes the good point that there is more to people than can be seen on the surface, but I think it is also a bit misleading.

It implies that somewhere, deep down in the middle, is the 'real' you, and these layers are somehow less real. I think all our layers are important parts of us, and some of the most important parts of our life are not deep and meaningful but the little everyday things that we do.

Furthermore, the metaphor makes it sound as though people are static, fixed things, and that can encourage the problems around nominalizations that we talked about earlier.

I think that we are all on a journey through life and as we travel on that journey we evolve. We are not like the middle of an onion but rather we are living creatures who learn and adapt and change as we get older. From this point of view, getting to know your partner is not so much like finding the kernel at the centre of the onion but more like having a long-term travelling companion, and as you travel both of you respond to your environment and learn and grow.

Assumptions

When you first meet someone you like, it is natural to be kind and helpful and generous and to show them your best side. As two individuals move into a long-term relationship, they show each other more and more of their natural, everyday behaviour. On the one hand, the relationship is a chance to up your game and show your best side more often. On the other hand, it is a challenge to get to know and love the less-than-best side of your partner.

As a relationship proceeds, sooner or later we become aware of the assumptions we have brought to it. Most of us learn about relationships in our family of origin. Whatever environment you are raised in is normal to you, and so that is what you expect when you grow up. It is only when our expectations are not met that we notice how much we assume about people. That is when we find out that what we think is 'normal' or 'what everyone does' is in fact just 'normal for me' and 'what some people do'.

Each family is different. Some families love to have celebrations. They have a party for every birthday in the family. They have feasts at Christmas and New Year and birthdays and any other time they find a reason for celebrating – a new job, a graduation, a farewell party, a welcome-back party. Some families just love parties. Others don't. A friend of mine married into a party-loving family. On his new wife's birthday, he gave her a present, he bought her flowers and he cooked her dinner. Over dinner she burst into tears and accused him of being ashamed of her. He told me he felt like he'd been slapped in the face. He felt as though she didn't give a damn about his present, the flowers and the dinner, but he made a huge effort and managed not to lose his temper. Instead he asked her what made her think he was ashamed. It turned out that as he had not told her in advance that he would arrange a party, she assumed he must be planning a surprise party. Then there was no party at all, just the two of them for dinner. She thought there must be a reason he had refused to have a party and all she could think of was that he wanted to hide her and their marriage away, so he must be ashamed. It is quite a leap to get from 'no party' to 'ashamed of your wife' but as she got more and more upset inside it made her think more and more upsetting thoughts, so she had gone into a spiral of doubt and anger before she burst into tears.

In her family of origin, you *always* had a party on a birthday. She couldn't imagine anything else. When it didn't happen, she didn't think, 'Oh, he's not like that.' It was more natural for her to assume there must be a reason, and it had to be serious and bad.

In his family, things were very different. The family was kind and loving, but they rarely had parties. In his family they liked cooking and conversation so that was how they showed their love. When they finally sorted it all out, they were able to laugh about it, and over time they have had plenty of nice dinners together and he has learned how to throw a great party.

Getting to know each other

Two of the great benefits of a relationship are first that we get to know our partners better and better, and secondly that we get to know ourselves better.

All the ideas and feelings and history that you bring affect you both, but they do not determine your relationship. They are your raw material. As you spend time together, different elements of yourself come to the surface and the work of your relationship is meeting all these parts of each other, whether known or unknown, with compassion, energy and honesty. All this stuff is the buried treasure of your relationship. As time passes, you will find more and more of it and find out more about yourselves and each other.

I have a good friend who is now in the happiest relationship he has ever had. He used to flit from one relationship to another and he seemed to get bored very quickly. Nowadays he tells me that he is still interested in variety, but instead of continually meeting new people, he now finds infinite variety in the same person. He compares his partner to a Mandelbrot set. A Mandelbrot set is a mathematical equation that generates a beautiful image that is infinitely deep. You can zoom in and zoom in and zoom in and it carries on expanding and showing more and more detail.

Sharing

One of the joys of a relationship is sharing experiences with your partner. It is more fun to go to a movie with your partner than on your own, more fun to cook and eat together than dining solo, more fun to holiday with a lover than alone. Sharing is a good thing, but like all things it can be misunderstood.

I talked to a young woman who had recently got married and she told me that she was worried that her husband was getting bored with her. I was puzzled because when I saw them together he looked happy, but she told me that he liked to do things on his own. As we talked it become clear that, in her mind, since they were married they should now do everything together whenever possible. I asked her why she thought that. She looked puzzled. To her 'sharing everything' was the definition of marriage. Her belief was that married people should be together, stick together and share everything. Maybe that works for some people, but it was clear that it was not what her husband thought. He seemed very happy to be with her, but he was also happy to spend some time apart from her. I suggested that some time when they were relaxed and had some free time, they should talk about their expectations and what might be the right amount of 'together time'.

Another woman told me of a different frustration with her partner. She told me that he didn't share feelings with her. It is a very old-school type of complaint that men don't share their feelings, but as she explained her situation it turned out that that was not what she meant. He often did actually tell her what he felt about things, and he was willing to be vulnerable and admit his mistakes. Her complaint was that when she told him how she felt, he did not feel the same. Once again, I was puzzled. So, I asked her what she imagined ought to happen. She believed that if she was angry and she shared her feelings, he too should be angry. She thought that the right way to share feelings in a relationship was 'feeling the same feelings'.

Well, sometimes that happens, but most of the time it doesn't. Mostly 'sharing your feelings' means expressing them honestly so that the other person knows how you really feel. It does not mean that you both have to feel the same thing.

If my partner is feeling bad, I will be sad about that, but that doesn't mean I know exactly how they feel. It means I have sympathy for them. How another person feels depends on their makeup and their reactions. One of the great advantages of a relationship is that very often your partner does not feel the same, because they have a different point of view, and that can help you to escape from feeling bad.

Getting insight into who you really are

It can be quite a surprise to find that the person you can learn most about in a relationship is not your partner but yourself. We all have blind spots and by definition we can't see them. We don't know what we don't know. Some blind spots are created because our unconscious mind is trying to protect us from uncomfortable feelings.

Other blind spots are accidental and they are not all traumatic. A friend of mine went to a boarding school and on his first half-term he went with his scout troop on a camping expedition. After supper on the first night, he was given the task of washing up the pots and pans. He rinsed them in water, wiped them down and put them on the rack. The scoutmaster gave them back to him and told him to do the job properly. He had to confess he didn't know what to do. He wasn't lazy, he just had never done the washing-up before. All of us have holes in our education somewhere and in the close quarters of a relationship, sooner or later they come to light.

BUTTONS

As we get intimate, we share our secrets and show our weaknesses. That trust and closeness produces a special glow of togetherness. Unfortunately, no couple is perfect and inevitably there will be times when you disagree. The part of you, or your partner, that wants to fight knows exactly where to wound you most. It knows the most hurtful things to say. Hurtful words are apt to trigger defensiveness and that tends to make arguments worse. It is a great achievement to resist the urge to fight back, but if occasionally we manage to do so, we get a great reward. Not only do you defuse an argument or prevent a situation getting even more hurtful, but you find yourself face to face with your own sensitivity, you get to see very clearly what you value and you can also see your partner's position more clearly. Instead of getting lost and angry in a fight, you are free to ask how you can stand up for your values rather than fall into a row.

DEFENSIVENESS

Defensive reactions are mostly quick, automatic responses arising from the unconscious. We can't stop them arising, but instead of immediately acting them out, we can turn them into an alarm bell. If I am being defensive that means there is something I value being threatened. I have to consciously take responsibility to look after myself, then turn towards the defensiveness and ask, 'What am I defending? What is it that I value and feels threatened? Why does it need defending? What is a better conscious way to stand up for my values?'

As we saw in Question One, defensiveness is one of Dr Gottman's signs of trouble in a relationship. We can see here why that is. If I can stop being defensive, I can see my own values and sensitivities more clearly and I can begin to understand my partner better. When I give up being defensive, it doesn't mean I give in to every argument or do anything I am told to do. It just means I don't need to get into a fight about it. Sometimes it means I can have a rational discussion instead. Sometimes it means I can just stay good-humoured, let the matter drop and wait for a better time to discuss it.

LEAST DEVELOPED PARTS

Much of what we discover when we are hurt are simply good parts of ourselves that have not been allowed to develop properly. As I said earlier, when I was young I had my heart broken, so I spent decades stopping anyone from getting really close to me to protect myself from getting hurt again. Well, it did stop another heartbreak. It also stopped my relationships getting richer and deeper. Beyond that, it also stopped an important part of my sensitivity from developing. One of the reasons I was so stuck on the 'achievement treadmill' was because I wasn't very good at appreciating what I had. I was always hunting for something more. It turns out that appreciation is a capability we can ignore or develop. When I finally was able to be open in a relationship, it allowed me to appreciate all sorts of aspects of my life beyond my relationship. I don't need to keep seeking intense pleasure experiences because the overall backdrop of my life now is well-being and happiness.

Owner or victim

A few years ago, a friend asked me a strange question: 'Are you an owner or a victim?'

It made a great impression on me. I realized that in my business I was without doubt an owner. I fought for my achievements, I took responsibility for my mistakes and I made my own success. But when I thought about my series of short-term relationships, I realized I was thinking I wasn't 'good enough' to stay together with a loving woman for a long time. I was 'doomed' to end every relationship with fights and misunderstandings. I took all this for granted. It was the frame within which I thought of myself.

I dated many different women, but over and over again the relationships ended and more often than not with arguments, confusion and sadness. I soon had a series of experiences in my love life that convinced me I was a victim. I didn't say that word to myself, I didn't even think of it like that. I just said things like, 'I'm not built for relationships,' and secretly I was preparing to be on my own in my life.

Even when I was in a relationship I was sure the woman would end it and I would be on my own again.

I told myself a story and gave myself the identity of a victim of the women who took advantage of me. I imagined that there was something wrong with me, and I blamed the women. I believed they did it to me.

Perhaps a few years earlier I would have failed to hear my friend's question properly. I certainly would have rejected the world 'victim'. I was making the best of my situation and telling myself I enjoyed the freedom and the variety, and there was some truth in that.

However, when I heard the question, I realized that in my relationship life I was behaving as though I was the victim. I was complaining to my friend about the women that I ended up with, but he pointed out the common denominator was me. As we saw earlier, my unconscious was trying to protect me, but the price of that was that I became a victim.

As that thought became conscious for me, I realized I had a choice. As long as it was unconscious, I couldn't do anything about it. Now that I could see it, I could see the possibility of changing it.

I took responsibility for my decisions. Taking responsibility does not mean saying everything is my fault. Clearly, I made mistakes, but my exes made mistakes too. But it does not matter who makes the mistake or is at fault. If anyone 'did something' to me, I was responsible for letting them do it. When I took responsibility and recognized that I had a part to play in what happened, I restored my power.

I realized my choices were not my fault, but they were my responsibility. As I took responsibility for them, I could take charge of them. By taking responsibility for my own behaviour I can regain my power and change things for the better, regardless of what the other person thinks, does or believes. My friend's question was one of several events that made me aware of what I was doing, and that awareness was the first step towards changing it.

Victim, persecutor, rescuer

If anyone acts like a victim, they create two other roles: the persecutor and the rescuer. The persecutor is doing the things that hurt and make you a victim, and the rescuer offers a way to escape. Another way to put it is that the roles all require each other. You can't rescue anyone unless there is a bad situation from which they can be rescued. You can't be a persecutor unless you have someone to persecute and so on.

The big problem is that unless these three people learn how to look after themselves (Question Three), they will tend to keep looking for other people with whom they can play victim, persecutor, rescuer. Some people specialize in one role, but quite a few will move round the triangle, playing each role in turn. A classic example of this is when married people have affairs. My friend, let's call him John, had a beautiful wife and three great children but he began to feel like a victim in his marriage because his wife was always pushing everyone in the family to achieve more and more. He felt he wasn't getting the respect he deserved and he found it in the arms of a younger woman. She was his rescuer. When it all came out his wife thought that she was the victim, and her husband was the persecutor. That put her at risk of finding another person to be her rescuer.

The triangle of victim, rescuer, persecutor would keep reappearing until they decided to look after themselves properly first. When they did that, none of them were victims, so there was no need for rescuers and no role for persecutors. That doesn't mean that dealing with this sort of problem is easy, but it never helps to get stuck in any of those three roles. Perhaps this couple will stay married, perhaps they won't. If they do want to stay married, they will have to work with the energy of that disagreement inside the marriage and both take responsibility for their decisions to stay married.

The puzzle of co-dependence

Sometimes partners are so close that they never want to be apart. If that situation makes them both happy, that is wonderful. It is less wonderful if they feel trapped or they feel unable to cope on their own.

The situation where people are unable to cope on their

own and depend too much on the other is known as co-dependence. Co-dependence arises when people fail to look after themselves properly but focus all their caring on the other person. Co-dependent people are not used to looking after themselves. They have very little experience of being responsible for their own mistakes and their own successes, because they are too involved with other people to be clear about their own actions. As a result they cannot imagine their partners taking responsibility for their own mistakes and their own successes. If they leave the other person alone, they feel overwhelmed by guilt.

Co-dependent people look after their partners and expect their partners to look after them. At first reading that sounds reasonable, but there are two deep problems. One is that they expect their partners to look after them *too much*. They tend to measure the value of their relationship by the amount of care they get from their partner, so they have a tendency to ask for more and more. They offer more help than is truly helpful or necessary and they ask for more help than is healthy or possible.

The second problem is that no other person can actually look after you as well as you can yourself. Remember, you are the expert on you. You know what you actually need and you are in the best position to make it happen. That's why our third question is, 'How do you look after yourself?'

Co-dependence creates a trap of perpetual activity which is never satisfying, and if it goes too far it creates desperation.

Of course, one of the pleasures of a relationship is helping each other and being together, so a certain amount of interdependence is a very rewarding part of a partnership. However, if people don't look after themselves properly they can fall into co-dependence. When that reaches desperation level it is an alarm bell for the whole relationship. If you are at all worried that you might be affected by co-dependence or desperation, use the following technique to defuse it.

DESPERATION DESTROYER

You can use this technique any time you feel too needy, desperate or insecure. Read the technique through from start to finish at least once before you use it.

 I have made an audio track to guide you through this. Download it at **www.paulmckenna.com/downloads**

1. In order to practise the technique, think about a time in the past when you were insecure or felt you were too anxious or desperate.

2. Step back out of that memory picture so that you can see the back of your head and move the picture away from you.

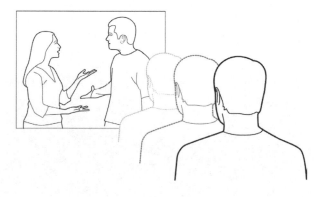

3. Drain out the colour, shrink it and make it dim and dull, and put it to one side.

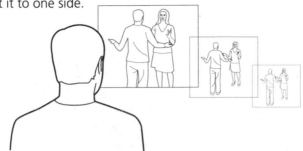

4. Now, think of eight different occasions on which you felt happy, loved, supported, secure, positive or successful. These times can be anything from a special smile with a loved one or celebrating a success or laughing with friends to winning a marathon. Remember what you saw, hear what you heard and feel what you felt.

5. Imagine a big cinema screen in front of you made up of nine separate boxes and put pictures of those eight wonderful, successful, loving times in the top two rows and at each end of the bottom row.

6. Take the first picture you made of the time you felt desperate and put it in the centre of the bottom row.

7. Now look at that time of desperation in the context of all this love and success. If at any time in the future you fear you might be needy or desperate, look at that fear in the context of all this success and love and happiness.

SUMMARY

BREAKERS

- **Unexamined inherited beliefs**
- **Being a victim**
- **Co-dependence and desperation**

MAKERS

- **Being an owner**
- **Learning about yourself every day**
- **Learning about your partner every day**

REVIEW: WHAT AM I LEARNING?

Now that you have read this chapter, I'd like you to ask the chapter question yourself. Take a little while to think back over the last few days and weeks in your own life or in your relationship and ask, 'What am I learning?'

➤ **Notice the times when you did or experienced any of the breakers.**

- *How did you feel?*
- *What happened next?*
- *What would you do differently now?*

➤ **Notice the times when you did or experienced or would have used any of the makers.**

- *How did you feel?*
- *What happened next?*
- *How can you have more of this in the future?*

Thinking now of all of your answers and the whole chapter, ask yourself again, 'What am I learning?' and notice everything that you have learned, small or large, and acknowledge your own success.

Now, in the 21-day relationship enricher section at the end of this book, or on your phone or in your diary, or even in a notebook, make a note of one area in which you feel, for whatever reason, that you would like to learn more, and make an effort to do so within the next twenty-four hours.

VISION OF THE FUTURE

•

Q7.
HOW ARE YOU SEEING YOUR FUTURE?

Q7. HOW ARE YOU SEEING YOUR FUTURE?

Relationships begin in many different ways. More people meet at work than anywhere else, but relationships can start online, in bars, through friends, on trains and planes and buses. Some people fall in love instantly, others take their time to decide. Some people fall into bed first and then gradually get to know and like and love each other. Not all relationships are high-energy dramatic romances. Some of them start quietly and grow slowly until gradually the couple feels more and more comfortable with each other. Some of us are surprised by love. Some people are happy enough dating and spending time with a boyfriend or girlfriend and only realize later, perhaps after a crisis of some sort, that they have grown to love each other.

The rose-tinted view

When you first meet your partner, whether you are brought together by falling in love or by fancying them like crazy or by a casual hook-up, you don't know them very well, but your imagination automatically fills in the gaps. The more you like them, the more work your imagination does. You imagine hanging out all weekend, going to a festival together or going on holiday. You think, 'My friends will love this person,' you might visualize beautiful scenes of domestic bliss or hours of mind-blowing sex.

We don't think, 'Oh, he/she is really attractive but I know nothing about them.' We think, 'Oh she/he is really gorgeous and my mum will love them, and we will have such a great time hiking in the Scottish mountains and paddling on the beach with our kids.' But in reality, we don't know if they even like hiking, or beaches, or kids.

The view from the past

It is completely normal to project fantasies on to our new partners. It happens automatically and it is inspiring and energizing. These fantasies come from the imagination and the memory banks of our unconscious. In other words, this is the future as seen from the past. We all inherit expectations and fantasies about the future that have been installed in us by the ideas and behaviour of the people around us in our childhood. We did not choose them. Some are idealistic, some are not good enough. We inherit ideas about how people should behave in a relationship, about what good people do and about how to raise a family. We can inherit much more specific ideas too, such as what people do on holiday, which political party is best or what is the right kind of food to eat.

When we fantasize the future of a relationship, our imagination takes all of these inherited ideas and throws them forward into the future. The whole process is completely automatic and, in my experience, there are two ways we can respond to it. The first is to see this projection as a template: 'This is what a relationship should look like, so we must do our best to get as close as we can to this pattern.' For a large part of our history it seems that this was the option many people took. Men followed the pattern of their father's behaviour and religion and often employment, and expected that women would behave as their mothers had behaved. Nowadays, few people expect to conform so exactly to the religious or working patterns of their parents' lives, but there are still often some less obvious expectations that emotional patterns will be replicated. The most common problem with this attitude is when the two partners have different and incompatible templates. If, for example, he expects her to earn a salary comparable to his and she expects him to provide all the money, a serious disagreement will arise.

The second attitude to the imaginative activity we inherit is to see it not as a template, but as raw material. All the ideas and projects are seen as possibilities, inspiration, and open to change and development. The great advantage of this approach is that there is all the room you need to include the fantasies and projections of both partners. When everything is an option, there is room for as many options as you can imagine, and then you get to choose together what to reject, what to use and what to develop.

Raw material

This attitude of seeing your fantasies as raw material has several advantages. It allows the recognition that both you and your partner are different from your respective parents, even though you may have inherited some character traits and expectations. We are not clones who must behave in exactly the same way as our parents; we are unique individuals with our own personal talents and preferences. Our family of origin was a kind of 'school for relationships' but it can only teach a certain amount.

There are inevitably gaps in the beliefs and behaviour you inherit. I worked with a man once who had a string of relationships but was convinced he would never find the right woman. As I enquired about his relationships, he explained that they all ended with arguments. That didn't seem unusual, so I asked a bit more, then suddenly I realized that he was telling me that if he had a serious argument, he believed the relationship had to end there and then, because to him it meant they were obviously not 'right' for each other. He did not know that a couple can argue, disagree and still maintain their relationship. I found out that his parents were from that time and class whose motto was, 'Not in front of the children.' He had never seen his parents argue, and so he had never seen them make up and carry on. He simply didn't know that was possible. It was a gap in his experience.

Control

When you decide to make changes, you will come across another factor. Hidden inside all your self-generated fantasies is the assumption that the fantasy naturally goes the way you want it to go, because it is *your* imagination, driven by *your* desires. In other words, your desires are in control of your fantasies.

Sooner or later, you discover that your partner does not have identical fantasies or identical desires. He or she may even want the same thing as you, but it may be in different amounts or at different times. Therefore, as your relationship develops you will find that you need to negotiate more and more with your partner. Perhaps you can persuade them to do what you want; perhaps you have to trade one day doing it your way for one day doing it their way.

During this process you will find out more and more about your partner's imagination and desires. A big part of being human is the ability to fantasize and be creative. These fantasies can inspire and guide us. They help us to create goals and to clarify what we want to achieve. All the inventions you can see in the world around you in science, medicine and technology were once just an idea in someone's mind. The same is true of every relationship. The better the ideas, the better the relationship. You may find your partner's ideas even more inspiring than your own, but it may also be that some of them will be just as unrealistic as yours. We all need to find ways to realize the best ideas that we share with our partners.

Do opposites attract?

It is common to meet a couple who have very different characters and interests, and that has given rise to the myth that opposites attract.

For example, my wife likes riding horses and motorbikes and I don't particularly like either of those. Her interests are different from mine. I am very happy in the limelight, socializing, and I can be a bit of a risk-taker in business. My wife is quieter and more grounded. Her character is very different from mine. In that sense we are opposites. However, I believe a key component in any relationship is that beneath the characters and interests are many shared values.

The other day we had dinner with a friend who introduced us to a couple who talked about how different they were. She is passionate and expressive and gets carried away with her enthusiasms. She has a vivid and striking personality. He is more reserved. He doesn't express his emotions a great deal. He has a background in engineering and is very methodical and observant of details.

I put it to them that for all their surface differences, underneath their behaviour they share the same values.

'Exactly!' said my friend and, after a moment's thought,

they both agreed. Their different characters were complementary and attractive to each other and underneath they had a shared vision of life based on their values.

Shared values

So, although superficially people say that opposites attract, in my experience I have found that the basis of a rewarding, functional relationship is when the partners have shared values. By values here I mean not just the things you enjoy, but the principles you respect and live by.

For example, I have a good friend who has a wife and several children and, much as he loves his children, he makes sure he puts his relationship with his wife first. He wants to show his children that his relationship is important because it is the basis of their security.

Whatever your values – family, religion, environmental, social – the more you discover and the more you share with your partner, the more you will build your common ground. You and your partner both bring dreams and aspirations to the relationship. Shared values help you decide which of them to choose as your practical goals.

It is quite possible not to know what your own values are, because until you get into a relationship you may not ever need to think about them. So, part of the journey of a relationship is discovering your own values. You may find that you have been living according to values that actually don't belong to you at all. They were the values of your society or your family of origin, and when you become aware of them you decide that they don't suit you. You can let them go. The same is true of your partner.

The pair of you have a journey together of discovering, exploring and developing your values. Your values must overlap but not necessarily be identical. You will also probably find out that you may share several values, but give them a different priority. Sometimes your partner's values will cause you to re-evaluate your own.

My wife is conscientious about environmental issues and I have become a bit more diligent about sorting out the recycling and so forth. This is partly because her values have influenced mine, but it is also because I respect her values and I know that it makes her happier to uphold them. In other words, I care because it makes her happier, and one of my core values is to increase the happiness in our relationship.

Clarifying and developing values

I have asked many married couples how they nourish their relationship. One couple had methodically talked through their values and how they wanted to live up to them in their lives. They actually came up with a list of what mattered most to them.

Top of the list was good health and right behind it was gratitude. They made a point of expressing to themselves and each other their gratitude for good health and all the other good things in their life.

Next came work. They both tried, as far as possible, to do work they valued or enjoyed for its own sake rather than just for the money. I try to do the same. Even though it is not always possible for all of us all the time, it is a very good aspiration.

The couple valued their friends and their freedom to travel and tried to organize their work to make enough time for both. In everything they did, they tried to express their values.

The following exercise is one of my favourite techniques. This simple process changed the course of my life, and I have used it over and over again with many different groups of people. Whenever I do, I always ask the group, 'Who got a worthwhile insight?', and every hand in the room goes up. In business, this use of imagination is called strategic planning and every company has to do it to survive. I call it 'Hindsight ahead of time' because it uses your capacity to imagine the future to help you to plan it. I invite you to do it with me right now.

HINDSIGHT AHEAD OF TIME

Read the instructions all the way through, and ask your partner to do so as well, before using this technique.

 I have made an audio track to guide you through this. Download it at **www.paulmckenna.com/downloads**

1. Relax and imagine going into the future, towards the end of your life.
2. I would like you to make the assumption that you have had an amazing, wonderful life. Now look back on the decades of your life, see all your achievements, your relationships and family, and all the wonderful experiences you have had, and ask yourself, 'What made it so wonderful?'
3. Make a list of the values that have made your life so wonderful.
4. Ask your partner to do steps 1, 2 and 3 as well.
5. Sit down with your partner and make a list together of your shared values.

FINDING LOVE

Our values can help us when we are looking for love. They can focus our search and they seem to provoke a sort of sympathetic resonance that can have almost miraculous results.

If there are two pianos in a room and you strike middle C on one of them, the middle C on the other piano will begin to vibrate. This is known as sympathetic resonance. It is a very good analogy for the amazing way in which human beings with the same kind of energy can connect. Your emotional state affects your entire body and all of the minute, non-verbal signals that we continually read in each other subconsciously. It is as though you are a radio station continually transmitting your own emotional energy all day long. When you are transmitting on a good frequency, good people will find you. In this way we find ourselves attracting or being attracted to people who have complementary or similar values. I believe this explains, at least in part, how people who have cleared internal blocks with Havening are able to begin or renew relationships with greater satisfaction and a deeper level of intimacy.

Back-engineering your route to the future

Your shared values underpin your goals for your future. Those goals are not necessarily fixed. For example, you might decide that you want your children to go to such and such a school when they are a bit older because it gets good results and you both like your friends' children who go there. But a year or two later, the school has changed. You will now look around to see which other possible schools you like. That's a fairly obvious example but some other goals are not so clear. It helps every now and then to review your goals in the light of your values.

Once you know your goals, however distant they are, you can 'back-engineer' the route to get there. Picture where you want to be and ask yourself, 'If I get there, what is the stage just before this one?' Work out what that is, then work out the preceding stage. 'To get there, what needs to have happened just before this?' Keep doing this, step by step, until you get to a step which is accessible to you from right here, right now. Now you have your route.

For example, imagine the values you share with your partner are a love of nature, peace and quiet, so you decide you want to live in a cottage deep in the countryside. Maybe you need to retrain to do jobs that are based in the countryside. Maybe your first step towards that could be finding an organization that provides working experience on a farm. It could be you discover you don't like working on a farm. That is helpful because it shows you what you don't want to do, so you can refine your goal. You may discover that you value friends and social life so much that you don't want to be so far away in the countryside. You have discovered another value so you change your goal to living somewhere with nature and greenery but closer to your friends. The goal is different, but the core values remain the same.

There are many steps and many alternative routes to that goal, but you can see in principle how you can work backwards and break it down, step by step, until you know what you have to do today to move towards your goal.

I have created a technique that provides a structure for this process.

BEST YEAR EVER

Please read all the way through before you start to use the technique.

 I have made an audio track to guide you through this. Download it at **www.paulmckenna.com/downloads**

1. Imagine it is a year in the future and you have had your best year ever.
2. Take time to notice what makes it so wonderful.
3. What has happened in your health?
4. What has happened in your relationships, personal and professional?
5. What has happened in your career?
6. What has happened in your finances?
7. What has happened that makes you so happy?

Goals and values

Sometimes your values are clear but you don't have a big, long-term goal. If you don't have a goal, you do need a direction. Earlier in my career I was very goal-oriented and each time I reached a goal I created a new one. Goal-setting helped me a lot, but more recently I have found I don't need to do it. I find it more satisfying now to ask a simple question: 'Am I living my values today?'

I ask:

'Do I feel healthy?'

'Do I feel loved?'

'Am I being loving?'

'Am I being creative?'

'Am I doing worthwhile work?'

'Am I doing something to meet my partner's needs?'

Those are the ingredients of happiness. If I can tick those boxes, I am living a worthwhile life.

THE QUALITY OF VALUES

There is an old saying, 'Love conquers all.' It sounds noble, inspiring and romantic, and it is all of those things. It is also ambiguous. You could read it to mean, 'Love is a force that is so strong that it will make everything work out well no matter what I do.' Or it can mean, 'When lovers truly love each they will do whatever it takes to overcome problems and ensure they are safe and happy together.'

There is a big difference between these two meanings. The first implies that love will do all the hard work for me. The second says that I am willing to do the hard work, because I love.

Most of the time life is not hard work and love is a stardust that makes the most ordinary things delightful. When you are connected to your feeling of love then something as simple as going for a walk with your lover can be the best thing in the world. But at other times life is difficult. No matter what your background, your wealth, your age or any other factor, life will send challenges to your relationship. You can use the questions and techniques in this system to help you at those times, and in particular you will find it useful to have a bright vision of your future together founded in your shared values.

Does it matter which values you share? Well, yes and no. If we consider simply the strength of the bond of the relationship, it doesn't matter what the values are so long as both partners share them. However, if we also look at the outcome then it does matter which values we hold.

For example, a couple who are possessive and jealous of each other can have a very strong relationship, although they are also likely to experience a lot of anger and frustration and fear and tension. A couple who are both envious of other people will have a lot in common and can spend a lot of time criticizing and belittling other people. Again, this is a strong bond but it doesn't generate much happiness. People who are downright evil can have a very strong bond, but that sort of relationship does not create happiness.

I believe a good relationship generates and promotes happiness, so I think that the values do matter. Two qualities seem to characterize the set of values which create positive relationships: optimism and compassion.

Optimism

Optimism is one of the most powerful creators of happiness. Optimism is not a point of view. It is a perceptual filter.

Furthermore, when your filter is optimism, you create a positive-feedback loop. Optimism helps you to see positive experiences and good opportunities, even in difficult times. You are more likely to take up those opportunities, so you have a positive effect on the world around you and you bring good things into your life. When you are optimistic, you really do change your own world for the better.

Optimism is, in the most general way, the perceptual filter of a positive future. Optimism allows us to see any current problem as a step on the ladder towards better times and greater fulfilment. The hypnotic trance (see page 26) will help you to adjust your perceptual filters in ways that make you more optimistic.

A wonderful example of optimism is a war veteran with whom I worked to deal with chronic pain. His injuries meant that he is now a wheelchair-user, but his optimism helped him to appreciate that he was not dead, he still had all his senses, and not being able to use his legs made him all the more focused on what he could do.

Compassion

Compassion is an important quality in relationships, first and foremost because we need to be compassionate to ourselves and to our partners. We all get things wrong occasionally. We make mistakes and sometimes we might upset other people. We mostly do this by accident or oversight but our actions are still our responsibility. That is where compassion helps. The kinder we are to ourselves, the easier it is to be kind to others.

Equally, your partner, however wonderful and lovely they are, will also make mistakes. Compassion helps us to accept that, to forgive any hurt caused and to continue to express love. It is not always easy, but the more you do it, the more strength you gain to do it the next time it is necessary.

Finally, we need compassion because human beings are fundamentally herd animals. We need to cooperate for our basic survival. Many people are quietly suffering from all sorts of problems, some visible, some hidden. The more we are compassionate and optimistic, the more we increase the general happiness in the world. One of my all-time favourite quotations is from the Dalai Lama who said, 'Kindness is my religion.'

The key to judging values is to look at the outcome. Worthwhile values generate positive outcomes.

Evolution

Relationships, like the rest of life, are an ongoing journey and on that journey your likes and dislikes change. Maybe you had a sweet tooth as a child and now you dislike sweets. Maybe you hated broccoli when you were at school and now it is your favourite vegetable.

Your preferences may change. At school maybe your goal was to be in the football team or maybe the most important thing was to be in the coolest gang. If you are a teenager or young adult your hormones make you very focused on having sex. When you first become a parent your tiredness makes you very keen on sleep. As your life situation changes, your goals change.

Along with the goals thrown at you by your environment, you have a variable amount of time to choose your own specific goals. Relationships flourish when partners have both personal goals and shared goals. Having a personal goal gives you your own responsibility, which is not dependent on your partner. Regardless of what time they have available, you can work towards your goal. Recognizing your own needs and setting goals to meet them is part of looking after yourself properly. Having shared goals creates tasks that you do together and that brings its own, different rewards.

All the goals that reward you are founded in your values, and your values can also change and evolve. It is helpful to check regularly that your goals conform to your values and to check whether you need to update your values too.

After my heart was broken when I was much younger I couldn't really get close to my girlfriends and as a result I didn't take relationships seriously. I liked to have a girlfriend but I didn't want to be limited – as I thought of it at the time. I was into having fun with this person now, and the idea of a different, equally fun partner in the future was attractive. I thought that freedom was a good thing.

As I got older my values changed. Nowadays I am aware that along with that freedom comes aloneness. If you jump from one relationship to another, as I did, you never get to have a really close companion. I still enjoy fun and beauty and excitement but I have also come to value the depth and intimacy of a long-term relationship.

Moving away from failure

No one has a perfect childhood, and for some of us that is quite an understatement. Some people have plenty of good reasons to want to be as unlike their parents as possible. I worked with a young woman who had body dysmorphia. When she was a child, her mother had left her and her father, and the father had turned to drink. He became a nasty alcoholic. He said truly awful things to this woman when she was just a little girl, and because it was said by her own father with such authority it affected her with the power of hypnosis. He told her what a bitch she was, how terrible women were, and how vile her mother was. When I met her, this young woman did not know how to think of herself as valuable, confident or loveable. That was the cause of her body dysmorphia. She hated the person she saw in the mirror, just as her father had. Once again, we see that the unconscious is purposeful but not logical.

She wasn't moving towards happiness. All her behaviour was about moving away from pain. She had no realistic sense that her life could be genuinely rewarding. Up to that point it was a struggle for her just to get away from feeling bad.

Everything had to change. She needed to focus on moving towards something positive, but in order to do that she had to have enough compassion for herself to think she was worthy of anything positive.

To help her change her sense of self we used the Eyes of Love, the Ultimate You and Havening techniques (Question Three). It was a huge step forward when she was able to look at herself in the mirror and not object to what she saw. She could appreciate herself and feel good. She had been dressing entirely in black for years, then one day she went shopping and she bought herself a white T-shirt. She told me, 'I don't understand – I just felt I had to get it.'

I did understand. It was a sign that she was ready to share

the brighter version of herself with the world. It was another huge step forward.

Her case was quite extreme, but in less dramatic ways I meet many people who are driven by a need to move away from failure, away from pain and away from people they dislike. Of course, it is often a good idea to move away from pain, but it does not give you any specific direction. To achieve a sense of satisfaction we need to have a positive direction. Rather than be driven by 'moving away', we need to move towards something we value.

Moving towards success

A friend of mine worked for a great theatrical director who told him that, as a young man, he had been desperate to get into theatre but he had no training, no connections and no money. Every day he went and sat on the steps outside a famous theatre company and asked for a job. He kept sitting there, and asking, day after day after day, until they gave him a job in the wardrobe department. That was the first step in a distinguished career. And in spite of the fact that he sat still in the same place for days and days and days, it is also a great example of the power of 'moving towards'. He knew where he wanted to go and his relentless pushing towards his goal created a path where there had been no obvious opening at all.

Perfectionism

I believe it is important to have something to be heading for, but it is equally important to enjoy the journey and not to wait for things to be perfect before you start enjoying yourself. I do not believe there is a relationship which is perfect all the time, but it's possible to have one that's perfectly wonderful just as it is.

When the internet started to become popular in the 1990s, when people would mainly communicate by text, not Skype, a friend of mine joined a discussion group and got into a conversation with an interesting woman. Over the next few months they struck up a friendship.

They got to know each other by text and then phone, and he had a sense that they had shared values. She lived in a different country from him, so they met somewhere equidistant. As soon as he saw her in the flesh, he knew this was the woman with whom he wanted to spend the rest of his life. They were sitting in a café and he said, 'Excuse me, I'll just be a few minutes.'

He ran down the road, found a jeweller, bought a ring, brought it back and there in the café went down on one knee and asked her to marry him. She said yes, and they are still happily married. It sounds like a fairy tale, but it's the truth. A romantic story like that is a wonderful start, but it does not mean their relationship has to be perfect every day. Every couple has their ups and downs and there is something beautiful about enjoying bumping along through ordinary, everyday life as well as having amazing romantic highs.

A good friend of mine, a very intelligent and accomplished man, married in his forties. One evening at dinner he surprised me by saying he was glad he had married later in life. Rather than regretting that he hadn't met his partner sooner, the way he saw it was he was glad he had had plenty of experience before marriage, as it had given him time to realize who he really was and what he really wanted.

These two very different stories show that it does not matter whether you meet at sixteen or at sixty. What really matters is a willingness to take your chances when they happen. If you are true to your values and you take your chances, you may even look back and be able say, 'That was just perfect.'

All these stories of other people's love matches or amazing successes may seem a bit distant. Perhaps you are thinking, 'I don't feel very in love right now. I have a stressful project at work, and I don't feel attractive, and my husband/wife/partner seems to be all caught up in their own world and part of me just wants to hide away.'

That happens. When life is tough or just dull, we can all fantasize about the perfect stress-free life and the perfect, ever-loving, mind-reading, divine sex-machine partner, but everyone has those fantasies of complete freedom and no responsibility from time to time. And we know that is what it is: a fantasy. In fact, it even has a good side. It reminds us there are feelings and possibilities we desire that we have not yet actualized in our own lives. After all, when you are living a truly satisfying reality you won't want to escape from it into a fantasy. These fantasies can remind us to look clearly at our own values, then our goals, and make sure we are living our values and moving towards our goals every day. When we do that, even ordinary everyday events become more meaningful and rewarding because in each of them we live our values and move towards our goals.

Enjoyable efforts

Thirty years ago I went to an Anita Baker concert. Just before her last song, she said to the audience, 'The most important thing to me is my relationship, and a relationship is something you have to work at every day.'

Her words kept going round and round in my mind and I remember them to this day, but at the time I thought, 'That sounds like way too much effort.'

Now when I think about those words I agree with her, but I no longer think it sounds like too much effort. I do put effort into my relationship because I want to. I have discovered that the more I put in, the more I get out, and it always repays me. Sometimes I have to make an effort when I am already tired, or I don't want to, or I don't really understand the situation, but whenever I act in accordance with my love and my values, things turn out better.

Everyone who has children knows that, however much you love them, they can be hard work. In a way, a relationship is like a child. It is a new entity that you have created with your partner and you are both responsible for it. The better you treat it, the better it becomes.

Power of focus

I hope you enjoy reading this book and I very much hope you find the ideas interesting. However, I want you to get more than interest from this system. I want you to use it to bring more joy, love and fulfilment to your relationship now, and to any and every relationship you may have in the future. Maybe you never really thought consciously about the effect of your vision of the future on your present. Maybe at the back of your mind you are waiting for something to happen so that *then* you will be truly happy. Maybe you have just been a bit vague about your future. I would like to invite you to use this system now to make a real, visible change to your life.

I am often asked: 'If there was just one thing, one piece of advice you could give to people, what would it be?'

The answer is this:

You get more of what you focus on.

That understanding runs through all the work I do in all the different areas of success and personal development. It is also true in relationships. One of the greatest joys in relationships is giving and receiving love. My good friend Dr Richard Bandler has created a wonderful technique that helps couples fall more and more in love every day.

HOW TO FALL MORE AND MORE IN LOVE EVERY DAY

Please read the technique* all the way through before you start to use it.

 I have made an audio track to guide you through this. Download it at **www.paulmckenna.com/downloads**

Part One

1. If there has been a time when you did not feel love towards your partner, maybe you had been arguing or they just were not that attractive in that moment, bring to mind a picture of that time.
2. Float out of the memory so you can see yourself and your partner.
3. Shrink the movie of the time so it is a small picture.
4. Drain all the colour out of the movie so it's black and white.
5. Make it disappear.
6. You can do this with as many incidents as you want.

Part Two

1. Think of a time you felt really in love with your partner and return to it like you are back there now.

2. See what you saw, hear what you heard and feel how good you felt.
3. Make the colours richer, brighter, bolder and notice how strong the feelings are.
4. Keep going over this memory until you feel really loved and loving.
5. Pick two more memories of times you felt really in love with your partner and repeat the steps of Part Two only until you feel full of love for your partner.

* This technique is used with the written permission of Dr Richard Bandler.

SUMMARY

BREAKERS

- The view from the past
- The selfish view of the future
- Lacking a positive future

MAKERS

- Moving towards success
- Finding your shared values
- Falling more and more in love everyday

REVIEW: HOW DO I SEE THE FUTURE?

Now that you have read this chapter, I'd like you to ask the chapter question yourself. Take a little while to think back over the last few days and weeks in your own life or in your relationship and ask, 'How do I see the future?'

➤ **Notice the times when you did or experienced any of the breakers.**

- *How did you feel?*
- *What happened next?*
- *What would you do differently now?*

➤ **Notice the times when you did or experienced or would have used any of the makers.**

- *How did you feel?*
- *What happened next?*
- *How can you have more of this in the future?*
- *What more can you do to make your relationship rewarding and fulfilling in the future?*

Thinking now of all of your answers and the whole chapter, ask yourself again, 'How do I see the future?' and notice all the positive hopes and dreams you have, however small or distant, of sharing loving, rewarding times with your partner, and acknowledge your own love and optimism.

Now, think of one new, positive, fulfilling vision of your future with your partner and make a note of it in the 21-day relationship enricher section at the end of this book, or on your phone or in your diary, or even in a notebook, and in the next twenty-four hours take one step, however small, towards making that positive vision come true.

CONCLUSION

As I worked on this book, I reviewed the issues around relationships that have come up with my patients over the years. I also reflected a lot on all my own relationships and observed those of my friends, family and colleagues. I observed many patterns, but I never found two identical relationships. Your relationship, and every relationship you will ever have, is unique. Your relationship with your parents is different from your partner's relationship with theirs. If you get married four times, each marriage will be different. If you have ten children, you will have different relationships with all ten of them and yet . . . in all of your relationships, as we have seen, there is a common factor, and that common factor is you.

Furthermore, if you ever want to change a relationship, the only part of it that you can guarantee you can change is your part. Other people, ultimately, will always do what they want to do. That is why I have focused so much on what *you* can do to make your relationship richer, better and stronger.

Three facts

I was also reminded almost every day of three facts:

- **We are all different.**
- **There is no single set of rules to deal with all the challenges of life.**
- **I don't have all the answers.**

Therefore, this book is not a book of rules. It does not offer a framework or template for relationships. I think of it as a set of tools so that you can learn more efficiently. It is rather like giving a student a pen, a notebook and a laptop when they go to university. None of those is the answer to their exam questions, but all of them will help them discover those answers. And as your relationship is unique, your answers will be unique. I expect that most of them will be similar, if not identical, to most other people's answers, but they will also be different in ways we cannot predict. That is why your own understanding and your own responses are vital as you read this book.

My own experience has taught me that it is when I have had problems that my understanding has grown. I would not wish hard times on myself or anyone else, but I am grateful for the learning they have given me.

Modernity

In spite of all the changes and freedoms of modernity, the most common aspiration of people around the world is a long-term, loving, monogamous relationship, but a recent survey indicated that the average length of a modern relationship, including marriages, is seven years.

Relationships in the twenty-first century are easier and harder than ever before. They are easier because there is less pressure to conform to particular, rigid roles. Any two people, or indeed more, can be in a relationship, and they can do it however they want. It is harder because society no longer supports or protects or encourages any particular type of relationship or roles within relationships. So, if you want a relationship to last nowadays, you have to do the work to make that happen yourself.

It is not easy to make the most of a relationship every day, but the more often you do it, the easier it gets. And as your relationship gets stronger, you don't need the support of society. In fact, you become a positive force in the society around you, because as you and your partner bring the best out in each other, you are more and more capable of contributing to the world around you.

A new relationship

If you are not in a relationship right now, then I hope that when you meet someone new, you do so in a more powerful, confident and attractive way. Instead of asking, 'Will they like me?' I suspect that you will ask rather, 'How can I enjoy their company?' If you find many ways to do so, that is an indication it is worth pursuing that relationship a bit further.

Simple

Good relationships are simple. They help us to work together on the tasks of life and appreciate all its joys. Good relationships are not complicated. If your relationship feels complicated, go back to the beginning of this book and work through all the exercises and techniques again and again as often as you need to. Ultimately your relationship should be simple and rewarding, but it may take a little time to get there. Take your time and keep going. Do something every day to enhance your relationship and you will make progress faster than you expect.

Time

I also expect that your understanding will change and grow over time. Life, and every relationship within it, is a journey, long or short, and as we travel along, our perspective changes and we see things differently and our priorities change. I have shared with you my own experience of moving from a rather self-centred and goal-oriented person to someone who is more concerned with living my values every day, with exploring the inner world of getting to know one person more and finding there is always more to learn about her and about me.

Once you have learned all you can from this book, I sincerely hope you carry on learning more and more, because you can learn a great deal from your relationship about yourself, your partner and about life. It is a lifelong journey and I wish you well on it.

Missing

In a sense I hope you realize that there is something missing from this book. The missing bit is all the unique details of you and your life. Those details are more important than every bit of this book, because they are your own raw material. This book is a system, but without any raw material to work with, it is nothing. When you put your energy, your situation, your willingness and your love into the system, it will help you to make your relationship stronger and richer than you ever imagined.

Re-structuring your thinking

I have not written this book to tell you or anyone else what to do. My aim has been to help as many people as I can reach their highest level of functionality in a relationship.

I hope that you have seen in this book a number of the structures of your thinking, and that you also know how to change them if you want to get different outcomes. We all know, when we reflect on it, that happiness is not about stuff. Happiness is a function of how you relate to the world, how you appreciate what you have and how you appreciate the people in your life, and most importantly your partner.

As you use this system, it will open up more and more opportunities to appreciate your partner and bring you both greater happiness.

I wish you all the very best for all the many years to come.

Until we meet,

Paul McKenna

THE 21-DAY RELATIONSHIP ENRICHER

THE 21-DAY RELATIONSHIP ENRICHER

I invite you to ask yourself these seven questions every day and write down the answers in this journal. This is not an exam. It is a memory- and action-booster and a record of success. Scientific research has proven that when we write things down, we are far more likely to achieve them.

I have included 21 days here, but please carry on doing this for as long as you like.

When you have written your answers, if it prompts you to reread a chapter or to use one of the techniques, please do so.

I also recommend that you listen to the hypnotic trance (see page 26) for the first 7 days, and do the Havening exercise (see page 118) for all 21 days. Thereafter, reuse them as often as you wish.

DAY 1

Today I did a Havening session ☐

Today I listened to the trance ☐

How am I communicating?

What am I doing?

How am I looking after myself?

What am I giving?

Have I had a disagreement today? How did it go?

What am I learning?

How do I see the future?

DAY 2

Today I did a Havening session ☐

Today I listened to the trance ☐

How am I communicating?

What am I doing?

How am I looking after myself?

What am I giving?

Have I had a disagreement today? How did it go?

What am I learning?

How do I see the future?

DAY 3

Today I did a Havening session ☐

Today I listened to the trance ☐

How am I communicating?

What am I doing?

How am I looking after myself?

What am I giving?

Have I had a disagreement today? How did it go?

What am I learning?

How do I see the future?

DAY 4

Today I did a Havening session ☐

Today I listened to the trance ☐

How am I communicating?

What am I doing?

How am I looking after myself?

What am I giving?

Have I had a disagreement today? How did it go?

What am I learning?

How do I see the future?

DAY 5

Today I did a Havening session ☐

Today I listened to the trance ☐

How am I communicating?

What am I doing?

How am I looking after myself?

What am I giving?

Have I had a disagreement today? How did it go?

What am I learning?

How do I see the future?

DAY 6

Today I did a Havening session ☐

Today I listened to the trance ☐

How am I communicating?

What am I doing?

How am I looking after myself?

What am I giving?

Have I had a disagreement today? How did it go?

What am I learning?

How do I see the future?

DAY 7

Today I did a Havening session ☐

Today I listened to the trance ☐

How am I communicating?

What am I doing?

How am I looking after myself?

What am I giving?

Have I had a disagreement today? How did it go?

What am I learning?

How do I see the future?

DAY 8

Today I did a Havening session ☐

How am I communicating?

What am I doing?

How am I looking after myself?

What am I giving?

Have I had a disagreement today? How did it go?

What am I learning?

How do I see the future?

DAY 9

Today I did a Havening session ☐

How am I communicating?

What am I doing?

How am I looking after myself?

What am I giving?

Have I had a disagreement today? How did it go?

What am I learning?

How do I see the future?

DAY 10

Today I did a Havening session ☐

How am I communicating?

What am I doing?

How am I looking after myself?

What am I giving?

Have I had a disagreement today? How did it go?

What am I learning?

How do I see the future?

DAY 11

Today I did a Havening session ☐

How am I communicating?

What am I doing?

How am I looking after myself?

What am I giving?

Have I had a disagreement today? How did it go?

What am I learning?

How do I see the future?

DAY 12

Today I did a Havening session ☐

How am I communicating?

What am I doing?

How am I looking after myself?

What am I giving?

Have I had a disagreement today? How did it go?

What am I learning?

How do I see the future?

DAY 13

Today I did a Havening session ☐

How am I communicating?

What am I doing?

How am I looking after myself?

What am I giving?

Have I had a disagreement today? How did it go?

What am I learning?

How do I see the future?

DAY 14

Today I did a Havening session ☐

How am I communicating?

What am I doing?

How am I looking after myself?

What am I giving?

Have I had a disagreement today? How did it go?

What am I learning?

How do I see the future?

DAY 15

Today I did a Havening session ☐

How am I communicating?

What am I doing?

How am I looking after myself?

What am I giving?

Have I had a disagreement today? How did it go?

What am I learning?

How do I see the future?

DAY 16

Today I did a Havening session ☐

How am I communicating?

What am I doing?

How am I looking after myself?

What am I giving?

Have I had a disagreement today? How did it go?

What am I learning?

How do I see the future?

DAY 17

Today I did a Havening session ☐

How am I communicating?

What am I doing?

How am I looking after myself?

What am I giving?

Have I had a disagreement today? How did it go?

What am I learning?

How do I see the future?

DAY 18

Today I did a Havening session ☐

How am I communicating?

What am I doing?

How am I looking after myself?

What am I giving?

Have I had a disagreement today? How did it go?

What am I learning?

How do I see the future?

DAY 19

Today I did a Havening session ☐

How am I communicating?

What am I doing?

How am I looking after myself?

What am I giving?

Have I had a disagreement today? How did it go?

What am I learning?

How do I see the future?

DAY 20

Today I did a Havening session ☐

How am I communicating?

What am I doing?

How am I looking after myself?

What am I giving?

Have I had a disagreement today? How did it go?

What am I learning?

How do I see the future?

DAY 21

Today I did a Havening session ☐

How am I communicating?

What am I doing?

How am I looking after myself?

What am I giving?

Have I had a disagreement today? How did it go?

What am I learning?

How do I see the future?

CONGRATULATIONS

I send you all my very best wishes as you continue to invest in your relationship and reap the rewards. If you have found this 21-day relationship enricher useful, please don't stop! Please keep asking these questions and making a note of your answers, and watch the answers develop over time as your understanding, your rewards, and your love become deeper and richer.

Your friend,

Paul McKenna